T0148625

Books in the ABICS Publications Series

Badiru, Deji, **Consumer Economics: Time Value of Dollars and Sense for Money Management,** iUniverse, Bloomington, Indiana, USA, 2015

Badiru, Deji, **Youth Soccer Training Slides: A Math and Science Approach,** iUniverse, Bloomington, Indiana, USA, 2014

Badiru, Deji, **My Little Blue Book of Project Management: What, When, Who, and How,** iUniverse, Bloomington, Indiana, USA, 2014

Badiru, Deji, **8 by 3 Model of Time Management: Balancing Work, Home, and Leisure,** iUniverse, Bloomington, Indiana, USA, 2013

Badiru, Deji, **Badiru's Equation of Success: Intelligence, Common Sense, and Self-discipline,** iUniverse, Bloomington, Indiana, USA, 2013

Badiru, Deji, **Blessings of a Father: Education Contributions of Father Slattery at Saint Finbarr's College,** Bloomington, Indiana, USA, 2013

Badiru, Iswat and Deji Badiru, **Isi Cookbook: Collection of Easy Nigerian Recipes,**
iUniverse, Bloomington, Indiana, USA, 2013

Badiru, Deji and Iswat Badiru, **Physics in the Nigerian Kitchen: The Science, the Art, and the Recipes,** iUniverse, Bloomington, Indiana, USA, 2013.

Badiru, Deji, **Physics of Soccer: Using Math and Science to Improve Your Game,** iUniverse, Bloomington, Indiana, USA, 2010.

Badiru, Deji, **Getting things done through project management,** iUniverse, Bloomington, Indiana, USA, 2009.

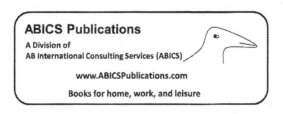

ABICS Publications

A Division of
AB International Consulting Services (ABICS)

www.ABICSPublications.com

Books for home, work, and leisure

Consumer Economics

Time Value of Dollars and Sense for Money Management

Deji Badiru

CONSUMER ECONOMICS
TIME VALUE OF DOLLARS AND SENSE FOR MONEY MANAGEMENT

Copyright © 2015 Deji Badiru.

All rights reserved. No part of this book may be used or reproduced by any means, graphic, electronic, or mechanical, including photocopying, recording, taping or by any information storage retrieval system without the written permission of the publisher except in the case of brief quotations embodied in critical articles and reviews.

The information, ideas, and suggestions in this book are not intended to render professional advice. Before following any suggestions contained in this book, you should consult your personal accountant or other financial advisor. Neither the author nor the publisher shall be liable or responsible for any loss or damage allegedly arising as a consequence of your use or application of any information or suggestions in this book.

iUniverse books may be ordered through booksellers or by contacting:

iUniverse
1663 Liberty Drive
Bloomington, IN 47403
www.iuniverse.com
1-800-Authors (1-800-288-4677)

Because of the dynamic nature of the Internet, any web addresses or links contained in this book may have changed since publication and may no longer be valid. The views expressed in this work are solely those of the author and do not necessarily reflect the views of the publisher, and the publisher hereby disclaims any responsibility for them.

Any people depicted in stock imagery provided by Thinkstock are models, and such images are being used for illustrative purposes only. Certain stock imagery © Thinkstock.

ISBN: 978-1-4917-5308-8 (sc)
ISBN: 978-1-4917-5307-1 (e)

Library of Congress Control Number: 2014920539

Printed in the United States of America.

iUniverse rev. date: 12/05/2014

Dedication

Dedicated to the time-based growth of money

Acknowledgments

I thank all my past students, research assistants, and teaching assistants of engineering economic analysis who gave me diverse perspectives on cash flow modeling, calculations, and analysis. Particular thanks go to Dave Sieger, Milan Milatovic, and Femi Omitaomu.

Contents

Preface

Time is the critical element in accumulating future values from a present cash flow value. *Consumer economics: Time Value of Dollars and Sense for Money Management* is a brief introduction to the manipulation of cash flows to leverage the power of interest rates with respect to the passage of time. "Consumer Economics" is a title created by the author to generalize the contents of the book for the general public. The title does not convey direct inference to conventional theory and principles of economics. The contents are simplified and pared down adaptations of the same methodologies and computational techniques used by large corporations, banks, lenders, investors, and global conglomerates. Money under the mattress, although flat in magnitude and hyperbolically declining in value due to inflation, used to be safe and secure in the bygone eras. Although that approach is still preferred by some people, it is advisable to put our money in interest-bearing bank accounts or other investment vehicles nowadays.

Most consumers don't understand why or how interest rates work over time. The goal of this book is to provide a concise guide to a better understanding of the time value of money based on the compounding effect of interest rates. The contents of Consumer Economics can help readers understand the underpinning theories and principles of different loan scenarios and cash flow profiles. Topics covered include cash flow diagrams, present value, future value, simple and compound interest rates, annual percentage rate, annuity, compounding of interest, capitalized cost, perpetual cash flow, rule of 72, payback period, benefit-cost ratio, mortgage loan analysis, and equity breakeven point.

The topic of equity breakeven point is particularly useful for analyzing when sufficient mortgage equity has been accumulated to offset the unpaid balance of the mortgage loan. Equity breakeven point is where the ratio of principal payment to interest payment becomes favorable for the consumer. In Consumer Economics, the usual mathematical complexity and jargons of economic analysis have been toned down to a consumer level to facilitate ease of understanding by readers. For those interested, one relevant general reference for the contents of Consumer Economics is the author's co-authored textbook listed below.

Badiru, Adedeji B. and O. A. Omitaomu, "Computational Economic Analysis for Engineering and Industry," Taylor and Francis/CRC Press, Boca Raton, FL, 2007. Readers are particularly encouraged to review the illustrative example provided on Page 29 of Consumer Economics.

Author's Credentials

Deji Badiru is the Dean and senior academic officer for the Graduate School of Engineering and Management at the Air Force Institute of Technology (AFIT). He is responsible for planning, directing, and controlling all operations related to granting doctoral and master's degrees, professional continuing cyber education, and research and development programs. In his post-high-school days, Deji worked as a graphic artist for children television programs, as a writer and columnist for community newspapers, and as an accounts clerk. These are practical skills that he frequently uses, even today, in his administrative and professional duties.

Deji Badiru was previously Professor and Head of Systems Engineering and Management at AFIT, Professor and Department Head of Industrial & Information Engineering at the University of Tennessee in Knoxville, and Professor of Industrial Engineering and Dean of University College at the University of Oklahoma, Norman. He is a registered professional engineer (PE), a certified Project Management Professional (PMP), a Fellow of the Institute of Industrial Engineers, and a Fellow of the Nigerian Academy of Engineering. He holds BS in Industrial Engineering, MS in Mathematics, and MS in Industrial Engineering from Tennessee Technological University, and Ph.D. in Industrial Engineering from the University of Central Florida. His areas of interest include mathematical modeling, systems efficiency analysis, and high-tech product development. He is the author of over 30 books, 35 book chapters, 75 technical journal articles, 115 conference proceedings and presentations. He also has published 30 magazine articles and 20 editorials and periodicals. He is a member of several professional associations and scholastic honor societies.

Deji Badiru has won several awards for his teaching, research, and professional accomplishments. Pertinent to the premise of this book, Deji won the 1994 Eugene L. Grant Award for Best Paper in Volume 38 of The Engineering Economist journal, awarded by American Society for Engineering Education (ASEE). He is the recipient of the 2009 Dayton Affiliate Society Council Award for Outstanding Scientists and Engineers in the Education category with a commendation from the 128th Senate of Ohio. He also won 2010 IIE Joint Publishers Book-of-the-Year Award from the Institute of Industrial Engineers. He also won 2010 ASEE John Imhoff Award for his global contributions to Industrial Engineering Education, the 2011 Federal Employee of the Year Award in the Managerial Category from the International Public Management Association, Wright Patterson Air Force Base, the 2012 Distinguished Engineering Alum Award from the University of Central Florida, and the 2012 Medallion Award from the Institute of Industrial Engineers for his global contributions in the advancement of the profession. In February 2013, he was selected as a finalist for the Jefferson Science Fellows (JSF) program by the US National Academy of Sciences and the US Department of State. Deji Badiru was the leader of the AFIT team that won the 2013 Air Force Organizational Excellence Award for Air University C3 (Cost Conscious Culture). His most recent award is the 2015 National Public Service Award at the Air Force Air Education and Training Command level. His most recent award is the 2015 National Public Service Award from the US Air Force Air Education and Training Command.

Deji Badiru has served as a consultant to several organizations around the world including Russia, Mexico, Taiwan, Nigeria, Ghana, and Canada. He has conducted customized training workshops for numerous organizations including Sony, AT&T, Seagate Technology, U.S. Air Force, Oklahoma Gas & Electric, Oklahoma Asphalt Pavement Association, Hitachi, Nigeria National Petroleum Corporation, and ExxonMobil. He holds a leadership certificate from the University

Tennessee Leadership Institute. He has served as a Technical Project Reviewer, curriculum reviewer, and proposal reviewer for several organizations including The Third-World Network of Scientific Organizations, Italy, National Science Foundation, National Research Council, and the American Council on Education. He is on the editorial and review boards of several technical journals and book publishers. Deji has also served as an Industrial Development Consultant to the United Nations Development Program. He is also a program evaluator for ABET, the international engineering and technology accreditation body. In 2011, Prof. Badiru led a research team to develop analytical models for Systems Engineering Research Efficiency (SEER) for the Air Force acquisitions integration office at the Pentagon. He has led a multi-year composite manufacturing collaborative research between the Air Force Institute of Technology and Wyle Aerospace Group.

Deji Badiru has diverse areas of avocation. His professional accomplishments are coupled with his passion for writing about everyday events and interpersonal issues, especially those dealing with social responsibility. Outside of the academic realm, he writes motivational poems, editorials, and newspaper commentaries; as well as engaging in paintings and crafts. As a contribution to sparking the interest of kids in science and engineering, Deji runs the Physics of Soccer website (www.physicsofsoccer.com). He is the founder of the Association of Military Industrial Engineers (AMIE). He also runs ABICS Publications, through which he publishes non-technical guide books for home, work, and leisure. A prolific researcher and author, Deji espouses the spirit of sharing knowledge freely and widely, which is the reason he offers self-published guide books to make his publications affordable and accessible to the general public.

Chapter 01

Time Value of a Dollar

Lighter Moment

From my own originally-composed witticism, I offer the following money perspective.

A suitor says to the lady he wants to marry, "I need to let you, I hate money so much."
The lady replies, "How come? Everybody loves money very much."
The suitor replies, "Money is the only problem I have."

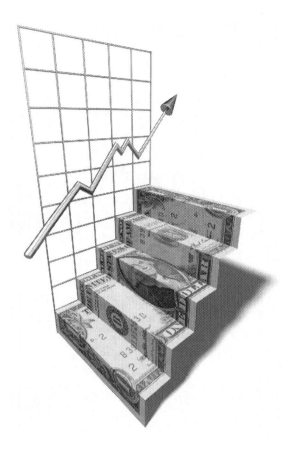

Time value refers to the growth in value of an asset over time. Time value of money refers to the higher future value of money due to the effect of an interest rate with respect to the passage of time. Time, in this case, is expressed in terms of interest periods, which may be years, quarters, months, weeks, or days.

Although the "dollar" is used as the basis for all discussions in this book, the calculations and the interpretations are equally applicable to other currencies, such as the pound, the euro, rupee, kwacha, krona, dinar, riyal, the won, the lira, the birr, the dirham, the franc, the mark, the yuan, the yen, the real, the cedi, the bolivar, the peso, the rand, and the naira. The techniques of economic analysis are applicable to any "coin of the realm" that is used and valued as legal tender in lieu of currency. The key is to understand money and how it grows in value over time under the effect of interest rates. In 1984, Jerry Greene, a newspaper columnist for the Orlando News Sentinel, wrote,

> "American are divided into two types --- those who understand money and those who don't. About 99.9 percent of Americans fall into Type B, including you and me."

The above quote was on the occasion of a cash flow analysis of the Professional Football contract for Steve Young of the defunct LA Express. The popularly-reported $40 million contract at that time only cost the LA Express $2.9 million to fund. Some of the deferred payments stretched into the year 2027, when Steve Young was to get a final $3 million payment.

The beauty of the time value of money can be seen in the case example of the descendants of Jacob DeHaven, a wealthy Pennsylvania merchant*. The family claimed that DeHaven lent $450,000 to the continental Congress in 1777. 200 years later, the family sued the US Government for $141.6 billion. In other words, with compounded interest and the passage of time, the initial loan amount has accrued to an enormous amount.

==============================

Another case example of a large professional sports contract gone awry is the case of NHL (National Hockey League) Blue Jackets player, Jack Johnson, who in 2014 filed for bankruptcy while blaming his parents for misspending his money. The reported nine-season contract of $18 million turned out not to be worth the upfront spending out of the contract. Jack Johnson claims that his parents spent far more money against his future earnings than the contract was worth. In other words, the money spent upfront was far more than the present worth of the contract. That is, the time value of money was not taken into consideration in the flurry of upfront spending. In order to prevent this

---

* http://www.nytimes.com/1990/05/27/us/213-years-after-loan-uncle-sam-is-dunned.html

kind of sad experience, the present worth of loans and spending should not exceed the present worth of the contract.

Another common example is how lottery winnings are paid. Lottery winnings used to be simply divided into equal payments to be paid over twenty years. Then, winners started suing lottery organizations for interest to be paid to them if the winning is not all paid up upfront. This resulted in the current practice of offering winners the cash option, which represents the present value of the advertised winning. The moral of this example is that a dollar today is not the same as a dollar tomorrow. A dollar today is worth more than a dollar tomorrow.

Consumer Economics is not an investment guide in the conventional sense. The focus is on computational techniques of cash flow analysis with respect to the time value of money. The focus of the book is not to provide a "how-to" of investments, but "how-to" for cash flow analysis, regardless of where the cash flow comes from. The book is not intended to teach you how to manage your money, but rather how to understand what is happening to your money as result of interest rate and the passage of time.

Chapter 02

The Sense of Money

Another Lighter Moment

From my own originally-composed witticism, I offer this additional wealth-sharing perspective.

A young married couple appears before a divorce judge.
The judge asks the wife, "What is your desired settlement from this divorce?"
She replies, "Your honor, I don't want to split!"
"How come, you brought your case to my court?," the judge says.
She snaps, "Sir, we can't afford to split because we have nothing to split."

As the saying goes, "money cannot buy happiness." The approach of this book is that even if money cannot buy happiness, it sure can facilitate it. So, it makes sense to accumulate it either through higher-income avenues or long-term dedicated growth of assets. All of this is for the purpose of spinning the wheels of happiness.

In a 2011 TEDTalk, Michael Norton, a professor at Harvard Business School (www.ted.com/talks/michael_norton_how_to_buy_happiness) contends that "money can buy happiness if you spend it on others." This author's view is that yes, indeed, having an opportunity to facilitate the happiness of other people can, surely, make you happy. If you practice it, you will discover that it is true. The key is to have an opportunity and the capital to do it. The relationship chart below illustrates how time and value create an opportunity. If capital cannot be achieved precipitously, as through lottery winnings, the best way to accumulate it can be via a time-value-of-money accumulation.

Booker T. Washington (1856-1915), an educator and author, said,

> "I began learning long ago that those who are happiest
> are those who do the most for others."

The availability of capital, over time, is essential for realizing the message in the above quote. The figure below illustrates the intersection of time, value, and opportunity to do something good for self or for others. Philanthropists derive joy from the happiness of others. On the other hand, those who subscribe to *Schadenfreude* (shadun-froi-de) derive pleasure from the misfortunes of others. This is not a good way to live a happy life.

Opportunity

Capital, in the form of money, is one of the factors that sustain business projects, personal facilitation of happiness, or pursuit of ventures in the enterprise of producing wealth. However, it is necessary to intelligently consider the sense and implications of committing capital to an opportunity (e.g., a business venture) over a period of time. The methodology of economic analysis helps us achieve that aim. The time value of money is an important factor in economic consideration of endeavors. This is particularly crucial for long-term projects that are subject to changes in several cost parameters. Both the timing and quantity of cash flow are important for managing financial resources and accumulating more wealth.

The evaluation of a project alternative requires consideration of the initial investment, depreciation, taxes, inflation, project lifecycle, salvage value, and cash flow. Capital can be classified into two categories: equity and debt. Equity capital is owned by individuals and invested with the hope of making a profit, whereas debt capital is borrowed from lenders, such as banks, and investors, such as shareholders. In this book, I explain the nature of capital, interest, and the fundamental concepts underlying the relationship between capital investments and the durations of those investments. These fundamental concepts play a central theme throughout this book.

Chapter 03

Financial Decision Processes

I emphasize here that The most sustainable wealth is the wealth that is accumulated over the long haul. Counting your dollars and watching them grow over time is an important decision. Financial decision steps facilitate a proper consideration of the essential elements of the decision that is made within the planning horizon of the decision maker. The essential elements include the problem statement stage, the information gathering stage, selection of a performance measure, selection of a decision model, and the implementation of the decision. The steps recommended for financial decisions include the ones listed below.

The Problem Statement

A problem involves choosing between competing, and probably conflicting, alternatives. The components of financial decision-making include the following.

- Describing the problem (goals, performance measures)
- Defining a model to represent the problem
- Solving the model
- Testing the solution
- Implementing and maintaining the solution

Problem definition is very crucial. In many cases, symptoms of a problem are more readily recognized than its cause and location. Even after the problem is accurately identified and defined, a benefit-cost analysis may be needed to determine if the cost of solving the problem is justified.

Data and Information Requirements

Information is the driving force for the financial decision process. Information clarifies the relative states of past, present, and future events. The collection, storage, retrieval, organization, and processing of raw data are important components for generating information. Without data, there can be no information. Without good information, there cannot be a valid decision. The essential requirements for generating financial information are suggested below.

- Ensuring that an effective data collection procedure is followed

- Determining the type and the appropriate amount of data to collect
- Evaluating the data collected with respect to information potential
- Evaluating the cost of collecting the required data

For example, suppose a manager is presented with a recorded fact that says, "Sales for the last quarter are 10,000 units." This constitutes ordinary data. There are many ways of using the above data to make a decision depending on the manager's value system. An analyst, however, can ensure the proper use of the data by transforming it into information, such as, "Sales of 10,000 units for last quarter are within x percent of the targeted value." This type of information is more useful to the manager for decision making.

The Performance Measure

A performance measure for the competing alternatives should be specified. The decision maker assigns a perceived worth or value to the available alternatives. Setting measures of performance is crucial to the process of defining and selecting alternatives. Some performance measures for financial decisions are cost, time, resource requirement, and interest rate.

The Decision Model

A decision model provides the basis for the analysis and synthesis of information and it is the mechanism by which competing alternatives are compared. To be effective, a decision model must be based on a systematic and logical framework for guiding financial decisions. A decision model can be verbal, graphical, or mathematical representation of the ideas in the decision-making process. Cash flow diagrams, discussed in the next chapter, constitute an example of a graphical decision model for financial analysis. A financial decision model should have the following characteristics.

- Simplified representation of the actual situation
- Explanation and prediction of the actual situation
- Validity and appropriateness
- Applicability to similar problems

The formulation of a decision model involves three essential components:

Abstraction: Determining the relevant factors
Construction: Combining the factors into a logical model
Validation: Assuring that the model adequately represents the problem

The basic types of decision models for financial management may include the following.

Descriptive models: These models are directed at describing a decision scenario and identifying the associated problem. For example, a financial analyst might use a cash flow diagram to describe the profile of an investment opportunity.

Prescriptive models: These models furnish procedural guidelines for implementing actions. An interest rate quote, for example, may be used to prescribe what is expected out of an investment.

Predictive models: These models are used to predict future events in a problem environment. They are typically based on historical data about the problem situation. For example, a regression model based on past data may be used to predict future gains associated with a business venture. Predictive models are common in the stock market.

Satisficing models: These models provide trade-off strategies for achieving satisfactory solutions to problems within given constraints. Goal programming and other multi-criteria techniques provide good satisficing solutions. For example, these models are helpful in cases where time limitations, resource shortages, and performance requirements constrain the implementation of a decision.

Optimization models: These are mathematical models that are designed to find the best available solution to a problem subject to a certain set of constraints. For example, an optimization model can be used to determine the optimal investment mix for a capital investment opportunity.

In many situations, two or more of the above models may be involved in the solution of a problem. For example, a descriptive model might provide insights into the nature of the problem; an optimization model might provide the optimal set of actions to take in solving the problem; a satisficing model might temper the optimal solution with reality; and a predictive model might predict the expected outcome of implementing the solution.

Making the Decision

Using the available data, information, and the decision model, the decision maker will determine the real-world actions that are needed to solve the stated problem. A sensitivity analysis may be useful for determining what changes in parameter values might cause a change in the decision.

Implementing the Decision

A decision represents the selection of an alternative that satisfies the objective stated in the problem statement. A good decision is useless until it is implemented. An important aspect of a decision is to specify how it is to be implemented. Selling the decision to others requires a well-organized persuasive presentation. The way a decision is presented can directly influence whether or not it is adopted. Once a decision is implemented, it needs to be monitored and tracked to ensure that it is yielding what is expected out of it. The next chapters present some tools and techniques of conducting economic analysis and making a financial decision.

Chapter 04

Cash Flow Diagrams

A cash flow diagram presents a visual representation of economic transactions. Seeing a clear picture of when and where funds are located within the planning horizon, helps to have a better understanding of the effect of interest rates on the time value of money.

With a cash flow diagram, you can show the timing, direction, and magnitude of cash flows. It is similar to an arrow diagram for statics and dynamics in engineering principles. The following conventions apply for cash flow diagrams.

- The time line is shown going from left to right.
- The starting point is often referenced as Point Zero (t = 0).
- An arrow head is used to show the direction of funds flows.
- An arrow going up shows money flowing in (income).
- An arrow going down shows money flowing out (expenditure).
- Although not necessarily drawn to scale, the relative size of the arrow indicates the magnitude of a cash flow.

Practically, the direction of the arrows depends on from whose perspective the cash diagram is being drawn. The direction from a borrower's perspective will be reversed from that of the lender. A cash flow example is shown below, with funds flowing in and flowing out over a number of interest periods. Increasing complexity can be achieved by loading up the diagram with additional arrows here and there. An ugly example is shown in the second diagram, which may represent how a savings account might be operated with a series of unstructured withdrawals here and there.

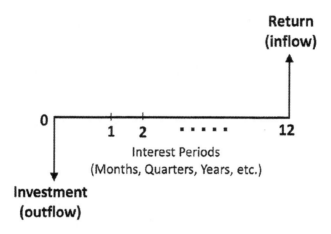

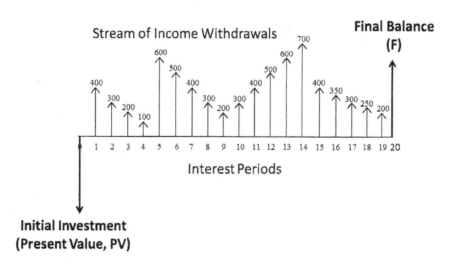

Chapter 05

Simple and Compound Interest

The computational vehicle for cash flow analysis is the interest rate. You pay interest on what you borrow and you earn interest on what you invest. A savings account is the most basic form of investment. Interest rates are used to quantify the time value of money, which may be defined as the value of capital committed to a project or business over a period of time. Interest rate is also referred to as the discount rate. Interest paid is the cost on borrowed money and interest earned is the benefit on saved or invested money. There are two types of interest rate.

1. Simple Interest
2. Compound Interest

The notations below are useful for calculation purposes.

F = Future value of an amount after so many interest-earning periods

P = Initial amount (principal amount, loan amount, etc.)

i = Interest rate per interest period

I = Interest amount (dollar value) accrued by P to achieve F n = Number of interest periods over which money is transacted

m = Number of times an interest rate is compounded per year (monthly, quarterly, semi-annually, or annually)

m = 12 means the interest is compounded monthly (12 times per year)

m = 4 means the interest is compounded quarterly (4 time per year)

m = 2 means the interest is compounded semi-annually (twice per year)

m = 1 means the interest is compounded once a year

m = 365 means the interest is compounded daily (365 times per year)

APR = Annual Percentage Rate, which is the effective interest rate based on the effect of how frequently the interest rate is compounded.

Simple interest is interest paid only on the principal; whereas compound interest is interest paid on both the principal and the accrued interest. Simply stated, compound interest charges interest on the accumulated interest, whereas simple interest does not charge interest on the accumulated interest. From an investment perspective, compound interest allows your money to earn more money because you earn interest on the accumulated interest. The power of Compound Interest is truly amazing.

Compound interest will yield a higher interest amount. In other words, the more frequently an interest rate is compounded, the more interest charges the consumer will pay on a loan. Conversely, more interest income is realized by the consumer from an investment whose interest rate is compounded more frequently. The figures below illustrate the respective calculation layouts of simple interest rate and compound interest rate.

Simple Interest

$$I_n = P(i)(n)$$

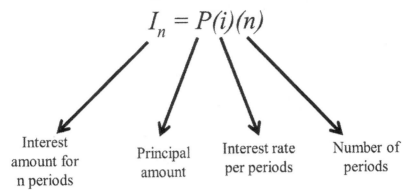

Interest amount for n periods

Principal amount

Interest rate per periods

Number of periods

$$F_n = P + P(i)(n) = P(1+ni)$$

→ Accumulated value after n periods

Compound Interest

$$I_n = iF_{n-1}$$

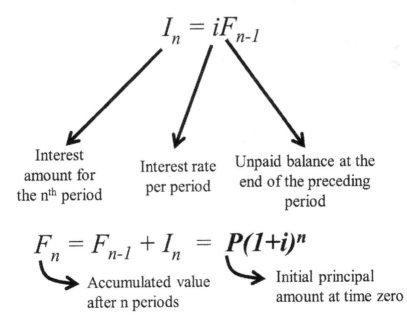

Interest amount for the nth period

Interest rate per period

Unpaid balance at the end of the preceding period

$$F_n = F_{n-1} + I_n = P(1+i)^n$$

→ Accumulated value after n periods

→ Initial principal amount at time zero

Simple Interest: $I = P(i)(n)$
Compound Interest: $I = F(i)$, where F is from the preceding period

Based on simple interest, $F = P(1 + ni)$
Based on compound interest, $F = P(1 + i)^n$

The F formula for compound interest is achieved by a series of algebraic back substitutions (not shown here) for F to reach the initial amount, P, so that the final expression for F can be in terms of P rather than the series of previous values of F. Algebraic back substitutions are the recursive processes of expressing a current value in terms of the immediate preceding value. This involves repeatedly applying a function to its own values iteratively.

Calculation Examples

Assume we have an initial investment of $10,000 paying a simple annual interest rate of 10% for a 20-year term. The future value of the investment at the end of the term is calculated as follows.

$F = P(1+ni) = \$10{,}000\ (1+20(0.10)) = \$30{,}000$

Now, if the interest rate is a compound interest of 10% per year compounded by year, the future value will be calculated as presented below.

$F = \$10{,}000(1+0.10)^{20} = \$10{,}000(6.7275) = \$67{,}275$

$67,275 compared to $30,000 is a huge difference. Won't you go for compound interest whenever you are investing? Won't you plead for simple interest if you are borrowing? I bet you will. Now, if the annual compound interest of 10% is compounded on a daily basis, the above calculation will be as follows.

$F = \$10{,}000(1+.10/365)^{365(20)} = \$10{,}000(7.3870) = \$73{,}870$

This confirms that the more frequent compounding of interest rate yields a higher investment yield. Please note that for calculations purposes, the interest rate percentage must be expressed in its decimal equivalent before plugging it into the interest rate formulas.

As a consumer, from interest income point of view, you want the compounding to be as frequently (i.e., higher) as possible. By comparison, from a borrower's point of view, you want your interest rate compounding to be as low as possible. The reverse is true from a lender's point of view. In summary, two factors determine the effective impact of interest rates:

1. The size of the interest
2. How frequently the interest rate is compounded

For the above reasons, a consumer should always inquire how frequently an interest rate is compounded when borrowing or investing money. If borrowing, you want fewer compounding periods. If investing, you want higher compounding periods.

Credit Unions, as member-service organizations, tend to compound savings account interest rates more frequently than commercial banks in order to serve their members more competitively. The following basic rules apply for a consumer.

Rule 1: If borrowing, a lower value of m is desirable
Rule 2: If investing, a higher value of me is desirable

Of course, in many cases, there are no options or flexibility in how the interest rate is compounded. The number may be locked in based on the generally-followed practice in the industry for the particular type of transaction being considered. Loans that are repaid on a monthly basis, by default, use interest rates that are compounded monthly (i.e., m=12). If not stated explicitly, the frequency of compounding is implied by the schedule of payments on the cash flow diagram. Thus, if payments are made on a monthly schedule, the compounding rate is monthly. If payments are made on a quarterly basis, the compounding is quarterly.

Creative manipulations of cash flow timing and interest rate compounding are the ways that financial gurus finagle investment effects. Professional athletic contracts often use convoluted cash flow arrangements that are confusing and befuddling to make a contract appear better than it really is. When such complex cash flows are discounted back to the present time, the upfront value will show a value lower than what is popularly reported in the Press.

Simple and compound interest calculations will yield the same results for F only when n=0 or n=1. The proof is provided computationally below.

If $F = P(1 + ni) = P(1 + i)^n$
Then, $(1 + ni) = (1 + i)^n$
Therefore, $(1 + ni) - (1 + i)^n = 0$
The above can only happen if n is zero or 1.

It can be seen that compound interest calculations represent a compound sum of a series of one-period simple interest calculations. Simple interest is not widely used in economic analysis. So, most clever manipulations of interest rates are done on the basis of how the interest rate is compounded.

Using the cash flow diagramming approach, the table below presents a summary of simple and compound interest calculations. The cash flow diagram presented for simple interest in the table is the same used for the compound interest calculations.

n Periods	Cash Flow	Simple Interest	Compound Interest
0	F ↑ / 0 ─ Time Line / P ↓	$F = P + Pin$ $= P + i(0) = P$	$F = P(1+i)^n$ $= P(1+i)^0 = P$
1	F ↑ / 0 ─ 1 / P ↓	$F = P(1+ni)$ $= P(1+i)$	$F = P(1+i)^n$ $= P(1+i)$
2	F ↑ / 0 ─ 1 ─ 2 / P ↓	$F = P(1+2i)$	$F = P(1+i)^2$
·	· · · · · · · · · · · ·		
n	F ↑ / 0 ─ 1 ─ 2 · · · n / P ↓	$F = P(1+ni)$	$F = P(1+i)^n$

Chapter 06

Effective Interest Rate

The effective interest rate is what your pocket actually feels, so to speak. As an analogy, the perceived temperature that the human skin feels is lower than the nominal air temperature based on the effect of wind speed. The wind chill factor makes you feel colder when the wind speed is higher. In economic analysis terms of borrowing money, the higher the speed of compounding of the interest rate, the "colder" your pocket gets. That is, the interest charges that you pay are higher.

The compound interest rate is used in economic analysis to account for the time value of money. Interest rates are usually expressed as a percentage, and the interest period (the time unit of the rate) is usually a year. However, interest rates can also be computed more than once a year. Compound interest rates can be quoted as nominal interest rates or as effective interest rates.

A nominal interest rate is the simple interest rate as quoted without considering the effect of any compounding. It is not the real interest rate used for economic analysis. However, it is usually the quoted interest rate because it is numerically smaller than the effective interest rate. It is sometimes quoted as the annual percentage rate (APR), which is usually quoted for loan and credit-card purposes. Depending on the desire of the source of the interest rate quote, APR is sometimes presented as the nominal rate and sometimes as the effective interest rate. So, a consumer must pay attention and read the fine print on how APR is defined. If APR is quoted as the nominal rate, then the effective rate after compounding must be defined as effective APR (EAPR). These definition nuances are the reasons that consumers get befuddled by the details of financial transactions and simply go with the flow without asking too many questions.

For the purpose of this section, the expression for calculating the nominal interest rate is as follows.

$$r = \text{(interest rate per period)} \times \text{(number of periods)}$$

The format for expressing r is as follows.

r% per year compounded per time period t
Example: 12% per year compounded per month

i% = interest rate per interest period
In the example above, r=12%, m=12, and i=1%.
$$r = mi$$
$$i = r/m$$

The effective interest rate can be expressed either per year or per compounding period. It is the effective interest rate per year that is used in annual computations for economic analysis. It is the annual interest rate taking into consideration the effect of any compounding during the year. It accounts for both the nominal rate and the compounding frequency.

EAR = Effective Annual Rate
Remember that sometimes, APR is defined as the same as EAR. So, pay attention to how the lender quotes the APR for you. Questions you should ask are:

- What is the annual interest rate?
- What is the nominal interest rate?

- Are they the same thing?
- How is the interest rate compounded?
- What is the effective annual rate?
- What is the annual percentage rate (APR)?
- Are they the same thing?

Note that many times, the person quoting the interest rate may not know the nuances and details of the interest rate types. So, don't expect to get accurate answers. He or she may simply be reading from company brochures without a deep understanding of the variables. You, as the consumer, will need to read the details, definitions, and interpretations yourself.

Effective interest rate per year is expressed by the following formulas.

$$EAR = (1+i)^m - 1 = (1+r/m)^m - 1$$

When compounding occurs more frequently, the compounding period becomes shorter. If the frequency approaches infinity, we have the phenomenon of continuous compounding. Although not used in practical economic analyses, this situation can be seen in fast-paced incessant stock market transactions. The effective interest rate for continuous compounding is computed by the following formula, which is derived by mathematically taking the limit of the EAR formula as m approaches infinity.

$$EAR_{continuous} = e^r - 1$$

Example

The nominal annual interest rate of an investment is 9%. What is the effective annual interest rate if the interest is

a) Payable, or compounded, quarterly?
b) Payable, or compounded, continuously?

Solution

Using the effective interest rate formula, the effective annual interest rate compounded quarterly is calculated as follows.

$$EAR = (1 + 0.09/4)^4 = 0.0931 \rightarrow 9.31\%$$

Using the equation for continuous rate, the effective annual interest rate compounded continuously is calculated as follows.

$$EAR_{continuous} = e^{0.09} - 1 = 0.0942 \rightarrow 9.42\%$$

The slight difference between each of these values and the nominal interest rate of 9% becomes a big concern if the period of computation is in the double digits. The effective interest rate must always be used in all computations. Therefore, a correct identification of the nominal and effective interest rates is very important. Consider the following example.

Example

Identify the following interest rate statements as either nominal or effective:

a) 14% per year
b) 1% per month compounded weekly
c) Effective 15% per year compounded monthly
d) 1.5% per month compounded monthly
e) 20% per year compounded semiannually

Solution

a) This is an *effective interest rate*. This may also be written as 14% per year compounded yearly.
b) This is a *nominal interest rate* since the rate of compounding is not equal to the rate of interest period.
c) This is an *effective interest for yearly rate*.

d) This is an *effective interest for monthly rate*. A new rate should be computed for yearly computations. This may also be written as 1.5% per month.

e) This is a *nominal interest rate* because the rate of compounding and the rate of interest period are not the same.

Chapter 07

Cash Flow Equivalence

Cash flow equivalence is the calculation of what a cash flow is worth at different points in time. A cash flow magnitude today is not the same cash flow magnitude tomorrow. A dollar today is not the same dollar tomorrow. To assess the relative performance of cash flows, all cash flows must be converted to the same reference point in time.

The basic reason for performing economic analysis is to provide information that helps in making choices between mutually exclusive projects competing for limited resources. The cost performance of each project will depend on the timing and levels of its expenditures. By using various techniques of computing cash flow equivalence, we can reduce competing project cash flows to a common basis for comparison. The common basis depends, however, on the prevailing interest rate. Two cash flows that are equivalent at a given interest rate are not equivalent at a different interest rate. The basic techniques for converting cash flows from an interest rate at one point in time to the interest rate at another are presented below.

A cash-flow diagram (CFD) is a graphical representation of revenues (cash inflows) and expenses (cash outflows). If several cash flows occur during the same time period, a net cash-flow diagram is used to represent the resolution of the inflows and outflows. Cash flow diagrams are based on several assumptions as summarized below.

- Interest rate is computed once in a time period.
- All cash flows occur at the end of the time period.
- All periods are of the same length.
- The interest rate period must agree with the periods on the time line.
- Negative cash flows are drawn downward from the time line.
- Positive cash flows are drawn upward from the time line.

Cash-flow conversion involves the transfer of project funds from one point in time to another. There are several factors used in the conversion of cash flows. The following notations apply here.

P = Cash flow at the initial time. This is usually time 0.
F = Cash flow value at some future time. This is usually time n.
A = Series of equal, consecutive, and end-of-period cash flow (annuity).
G = Uniform arithmetic gradient increase in period-by-period cash flow.
t = Time period measurement (days, weeks, quarters, months, years)
n = Total number of time periods (days, weeks, quarters, months, years)
i = interest rate per time period (expressed in percentage, but converted to decimals for calculations)

In many cases, the interest rate used in performing economic analysis is set equal to the minimum attractive rate of return (MARR) of the decision maker. The MARR is also sometimes referred to as the *hurdle rate,* the *required internal rate of return (IRR),* the *return on investment (ROI),* or the *discount rate.* The value of the MARR is chosen with the objective of maximizing the economic performance of an investment.

Compound Amount Factor

The procedure for the single payment compound amount factor calculates a future amount (F) that is equivalent to a present amount (P) at a specified interest rate, i, after n periods. This is calculated by the formula presented previously for F and P relationship.

Example

A sum of $5,000 is deposited in an investment account and left there to earn interest for 15 years. If the interest rate per year is 12%, the compound amount after 15 years is calculated as:

$$F = \$5,000(1 + 0.12)^{15} = \$27,367.85.$$

The table below illustrates the future values of an investment of $5,000 at different interest rates over different durations. Notice the rapid growth in the accumulated values as the number of years and interest rate increase. I could have been a multi-millionaire now if my parents had invested only $5,000 in my name 50 years ago at a fixed annual interest rate of 25%. Based on my humble needs, even 15% annual interest rate would have been okay for me!

$5,000 invested at i% per year for n years

n	5%	10%	15%	20%	25%
5	$6,381.41	$8,052.55	$10,056.79	$12,441.60	$15,258.79
10	$8,144.47	$12,968.71	$20,227.79	$30,958.68	$46,566.13
15	$10,394.64	$20,886.24	$40,685.31	$77,035.11	$142,108.55
20	$13,266.49	$33,637.50	$81,832.69	$191,688.00	$433,680.87
25	$16,931.77	$54,173.53	$164,594.76	$476,981.08	$1,323,488.98
30	$21,609.71	$87,247.01	$331,058.86	$1,186,881.57	$4,038,967.83
35	$27,580.08	$140,512.18	$665,877.62	$2,953,341.15	$12,325,951.64
40	$35,199.94	$226,296.28	$1,339,317.73	$7,348,857.84	$37,615,819.23
45	$44,925.04	$364,452.42	$2,693,846.34	$18,286,309.94	$114,794,370.20
50	$57,337.00	$586,954.26	$5,418,287.21	$45,502,190.75	$350,324,616.08

Present Worth Factor

The present worth factor computes P when F is given. The present worth factor is obtained by solving for P in the equation for the compound amount factor. That is,

$$P = F(1 + i)^{-n}$$

Suppose it is estimated that $15,000 would be needed to complete the implementation of a project five years in the future. How much should be deposited in a special project fund now so that the fund would accrue to the required $15,000 exactly in five years? If the special project fund pays interest at 9.2% per year, the required deposit would be:

$$P = \$15,000(1 + 0.092)^{-5} = \$9,660.03$$

Uniform Series Present Worth Factor

The uniform series present worth factor is used to calculate the present worth equivalent (P) of a series of equal end-of-period amounts (A). The computation is represented by the figure and formula below. The derivation of the formula uses the finite sum of the present values of the individual amounts in the uniform series cash flow, as shown below.

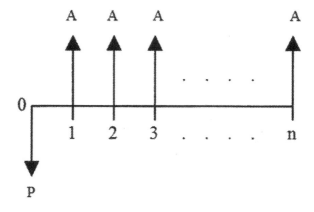

$$P = A[(1+i)^n - 1]/[i(1+i)^n]$$

Example

Suppose that the sum of $12,000 must be withdrawn from an account to meet the annual operating expenses of a multi-year project. The project account pays interest at 7.5% per year compounded on an annual basis. If the project is expected to last ten years, how much must be deposited into the project account now so that the operating expenses of $12,000 can be withdrawn at the end of every year for ten years? The project fund is expected to be depleted to zero by the end of the last year of the project. The first withdrawal will be made one year after the project account is opened, and no additional deposits will be made in the account during the project life cycle. The required deposit is calculated to be:

$$P = \$12,000 \; [(1+0.075)^{10} - 1]/[0.075(1+0.075)^{10}] = \$82,368.92$$

Uniform Series Capital Recovery Factor

The capital recovery formula is used to calculate the uniform series of equal end-of-period payments (A) that are equivalent to a given present amount (P). This is the converse of the uniform series present amount factor. The equation for the uniform series capital recovery factor is obtained by solving for A in the uniform series present amount factor. That is,

$$A = P[i(1+i)^n]/[(1+i)^n - 1].$$

Example

Suppose a piece of equipment needed to launch a project must be purchased at a cost of $50,000. The entire cost is to be financed at 13.5% per year and repaid on a monthly installment schedule over four years. It is desired to calculate what the monthly loan payments will be. It is assumed that the first loan payment will be made exactly one month after the equipment is financed. If the interest rate of 13.5% per year is compounded monthly, then the interest rate per month will be 13.5%/12 = 1.125% per month. The number of interest periods over which the loan will be repaid is 4(12) = 48 months. Consequently, the monthly loan payments are calculated as follows.

$$A = \$50,000[0.01125(1+0.01123)^{48}]/[(1+0.01125)^{48} - 1)] = \$1,353.82$$

Uniform Series Compound Amount Factor

The series compound amount factor is used to calculate a single future amount that is equivalent to a uniform series of equal end-of-period payments. The cash flow is shown below. Note that the future amount occurs at the same point in time as the last amount in the uniform series of payments. The factor is derived as shown below.

$$F = A[(1+i)^n - 1]/i$$

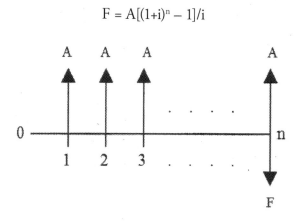

Example

If equal end-of-year deposits of $5,000 are made into a project fund paying 8% per year for ten years, how much can be expected to be available for withdrawal from the account for capital expenditure immediately after the last deposit is made?

$$F = \$5,000[(1+0.08)^{10} - 1]/(0.08) = \$72,432.50.$$

The example here shows how the uniform series compound amount factor can be used to assess and compare the future values of regular monthly savings of $20 per month over different durations at the interest rates of 5% and 10%.

$$F = \$20[(1+i)^n - 1]/i$$

For i = 5% per year, we have i = 5%/12 = 0.416667% per month. The formula then becomes expression below for i% per month expressed in decimals as 0.00416667).

F $= \$20[(1 + 0.00416667)^n - 1]/0.00416667$
$= \$4,800(1.0041667^n - 1)$

Using Excel spreadsheet, the above formula was calculated for various values of n.

Similarly, for i = 10%, we have 10%/12 = 0.83333% per month, which is 0.0083333 in decimals. The evaluation formula then becomes the expression below.

F $= \$20[(1 + 0.0083333)^n - 1]/0.0083333$
$= \$2,400(1.0083333^n - 1)$

The results from the above formulas are tabulated below. Notice the huge difference between the future values at 5% and 10% as the number of years gets larger. This is the power of the time value of money. If you have 70 years to spare and can put away $20 per month religiously over that long haul, you can amass quite a sizeable future value. The 100-year example may be for a city investing in a fund in anticipation for a future public service project. If the city of Dayton, Ohio has done this in the year 1914, the city could be reaping over $50million right now for city development purposes. Again, this is the power of the time value of money.

Years & Months	i = 5%	i = 10%
10 years (120 months)	$3,105.68	$4,096.87
20 years (240 months)	$8,220.78	$15,187.24
30 years (360 months)	$16,645.43	$45,209.19
40 years (480 months)	$30,520.97	$126,479.55
50 years (600 months)	$53,374.20	$346,480.90
60 years (720 months)	$91,013.84	$942,031.31
70 years (840 months)	$153,006.93	$2,554,204.61
100 years (1200 months)	$700,249.44	$50,713,383.13

Uniform Series Sinking Fund Factor

The sinking fund factor is used to calculate the uniform series of equal end-of-period amounts (A) that are equivalent to a single future amount (F). This is the reverse of the uniform series compound amount factor. The formula for the sinking fund is obtained by solving for A in the formula for the uniform series compound amount factor. That is,

$$A = F[i/[(1+i)^n - 1]].$$

Example

How large are the end-of-year equal amounts that must be deposited into a project account so that a balance of $75,000 will be available for withdrawal immediately after the twelfth annual deposit is made? The initial balance in the account is zero at the beginning of the first year. The account pays 10% interest per year. Using the formula for the sinking fund factor, the required annual deposits are calculated as shown below.

$$A = \$75,000[0.10/[(1+0.10)^{12} - 1]] = \$3,507.25$$

Chapter 08

Using Interest Tables

As can be seen from the preceding chapters, the formulas for cash flow equivalence analysis can be complex and ugly. Fortunately, all the cash flow conversion factors have been tabulated for ease of calculations. Some of the most-used interest rate formulas and tables are provided in the Appendix. The table below presents the relationship formulas and table entry symbols. Note that for table entries, the actual interest rate percentages are used. For the formulas, the decimal conversions of the interest rates are used. A common error is to forget to convert the interest percentage to decimals when using the formulas.

General notation for interest rate table conversion factor: **(Y/X, i%, n)**
Y is the amount being calculated
X is the amount that is given (i.e., known)
i% is the interest rate per period in percentage
n is the number of periods
Calculation format: Y = X(Y/X, i%, n)

It should be noted that interest tables are not provided for all interest rate magnitudes. So, the formulas are still needed for weird interest rates, such as 2.75%, 5.83%, and others similarly set values that the lender might use to discombobulate the borrower. If the consumer cannot pull out his or her calculator to assess the attributes of the loan, then the lender has a computational advantage as well as a knowledge advantage.

Table of Interest Rate Conversion Factors

Factor Name	Purpose	Symbol	Formula
Single Payment Compound Amount	To convert P to F	F = P(F/P, i%, n)	$(1+i)^n$
Single Payment Present Amount	To convert F to P	P = F(P/F, i%, n)	$(1+i)^{-n}$
Uniform Series Sinking Fund	To convert F to A	A = F(A/F, i%, n)	$\dfrac{i}{(1+i)^n - 1}$
Capital Recovery	To convert P to A	A = P(A/P, i%, n)	$\dfrac{i(1+i)^n}{(1+i)^n - 1}$
Uniform Series Compound Amount	To convert A to F	F = A(F/A, i%, n)	$\dfrac{(1+i)^n - 1}{i}$
Uniform Series Present Worth	To convert A to P	P = A(P/A, i%, n)	$\dfrac{(1+i)^n - 1}{i(1+i)^n}$
Arithmetic Gradient Present Worth	To convert G to P	P = G(P/G, i%, n)	$\dfrac{(1+i)^n - in - 1}{i^2(1+i)^n}$
Arithmetic Gradient Future Worth	To convert G to F	F = G(F/G, i%, n)	$\dfrac{(1+i)^n - 1}{i^2} - \dfrac{n}{i}$
Arithmetic Gradient Uniform Series	To convert G to A	A = G(A/G, i%, n)	$\dfrac{(1+i)^n - in - 1}{i(1+i)^n - i}$

Chapter 09

Capitalized Cost Formula

Capitalized cost refers to the present value of a single amount that is equivalent to a perpetual series of equal end-of-period payments. This is an extension of the series present worth factor with an infinitely large number of periods. This is shown graphically in the diagram below.

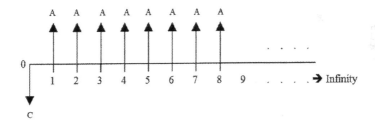

Using the limit theorem from calculus, as n approaches infinity (not shown here), the series present worth factor reduces to the following formula for the capitalized cost:

$$P = A/i$$

There are several real-world investments that can be computed using this idea of capitalized cost formula. These include scholarship funds, maintenance of public buildings, and foundations, among others. Some familiar inspirational examples are presented below.

- Rockefeller Foundation
- Carnegie Foundation
- Ford Foundation
- University endowments

Example

How much should be deposited in a general fund to service a recurring public service project to the tune of $6,500 per year forever if the fund yields an annual interest rate of 11%?

Using the capitalized cost formula, the required one-time deposit is calculated as shown below.

$$P = \$6,500/0.11 = \$59,090.91.$$

Example

A football stadium is expected to have an annual maintenance expense of $75,000. What amount must be deposited today in an account that pays a fixed interest rate of 12% per year to provide for this annual maintenance expense forever?

The amount of money to be deposited today is $75,000/0.12 = $625,000. That is, if $625,000 is deposited today into this account, it will pay $75,000 annually forever. This is the power of compounding of interest rate.

Reader's Exercise

How much would you need to set up a perpetual scholarship fund for a school so that $500 will be awarded every year forever, if the sustainable fund interest rate is 9.5% per year?

Permanent Investment Formula

The permanent investment formula is the reverse of capitalized cost formula. It is the net annual value (NAV) of an alternative that has an infinitely long period. Public projects, such as bridges, dams, irrigation systems, and railroads fall into this category. In addition, permanent and charitable organization endowments are evaluated using this approach. The NAV in the case of permanent investments is given by:

$$A= Pi$$

Capital Preservation

The basic principle of capitalized cost formula is to leave the principal in the fund account alone and live off the interest income. This is often referred to as capital preservation principle.

Example

If we deposit $25,000 in an account that pays a fixed interest rate of 10% today, what amount can be withdrawn each year to sponsor college scholarships forever?

Solution

Using the permanent investments formula, the required annual college scholarship worth is calculated as shown below.

$$A = \$25,000(0.10) = \$2,500.$$

The formulas presented above represent the basic cash flow conversion factors. There are many other aspects of cash flow analysis. But once the basics are understood, it is easy to convert to other cash flow scenarios. The cash flow equivalence formulas are available as tabulated conversion factors. Some of the most-used interest rate formulas, conversion factors, and tables are provided in the Appendix at the end of this book. Variations in the cash flow profiles include situations where payments are made at the beginning of each period rather than at the end and situations where a series of payments contains unequal amounts. Conversion formulas can be derived mathematically for those special cases by using the basic factors presented above. Conversion factors for some complicated cash flow profiles, such as the gradient cash flow series, are available in standard economic analysis textbooks. The case of the gradient series cash flow is addressed in the next chapter.

Chapter 10

Arithmetic Gradient Series

The gradient series cash flow involves an increase of a fixed amount in the cash flow at the end of each period. Thus, the amount at a given point in time is greater than the amount during the preceding period by a constant amount. This constant amount is denoted by G as shown in the diagram below.

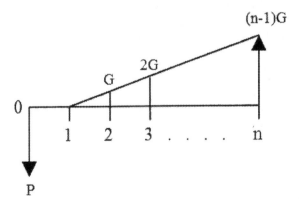

In the basic gradient series cash flow, the base amount at the end of the first period is zero. The size of the cash flow in the gradient series at the end of period t is calculated as follows.

$$A_t = (t-1)G, \text{ for } t=1, 2, 3, \ldots, n.$$

The total present value of the gradient series is calculated by using the present amount factor to convert each individual amount from time t to time 0 at an interest rate of i% per period and then summing up the resulting present values. The finite summation reduces to the general formula shown below.

$$P = G\{[(1+i)^n - (1+ni)]/[i^2(1+i)^n]\}$$

Example

The cost of supplies for a 10-year project increases by $1,500 every year, starting at the end of the second year. There is no supplies cost at the end of the first year. If the interest rate is 8% per year, determine the present amount that must be set aside at time zero to take care of all the future supplies expenditures.

Solution

From the data given, we have G = 1,500, i = 0.08, and n = 10. Using the arithmetic gradient formula, we obtain the following answer.

$$P = \$1,500\{[(1+0.08)^{10} - (1+10(0.08)]/[(0.08)^2(1+0.08)^{10}]\} = \$38,965.20$$

If we use the interest table, we will that the P/G entry for 8% and n=10 is 25.9768. So, we can directly calculate the above result as follows.

$$P = \$1,500(P/G,8\%,10) = \$1,500(25.9768) = \$38,965.20$$

In this case, the result agrees perfectly with the calculation using the formula. In some cases, rounding off differences may occur depending on how many decimal places are used during the formula calculation.

Gradient Series with a Base Amount

In many cases, an arithmetic gradient starts with some base amount at the end of the first period and then increases by a constant amount thereafter. The nonzero base amount is denoted as A_1 as shown in the figure below.

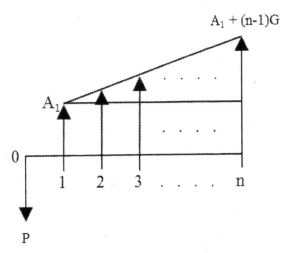

$$A_1 + (n-1)G$$

The calculation of the present amount for such cash flows requires breaking the cash flow into a uniform series cash flow of amount A_1 and an arithmetic gradient cash flow with zero base amount. The uniform series present worth formula is used to calculate the present worth of the uniform series portion, and the basic gradient series formula is used to calculate the gradient portion. The overall present worth is then calculated as follows:

$$P_{Total} = P_{For\ uniform\ series} + P_{For\ gradient\ series}$$

Arithmetic gradient series cash flows feature prominently in many contract payments but misinterpretation of them can seriously distort the financial reality of a situation. Good examples can be found in the contracts of sports professionals. The pervasiveness of, and extensive publicity attending, such contracts make the analysis of arithmetic gradient series both appealing and economically necessary. A good example is the 1984 contract of Steve Young, a quarterback for the LA Express team in the former USFL (United States Football League). The contract was widely reported as being worth $40 million dollars at that time [3]. The cash-flow profile of the contract revealed an intricate use of various segments of arithmetic gradient series cash flows. When everything was taken into account, the $40 million touted in the press amounted only to a present worth of the contract of about $5 million at that time. The trick was that the club included some deferred payments stretching over 37 years (1990-2027) at a 1984 present cost of only $2.9 million. The deferred payments were reported as being worth $34 million, which was the raw sum of the amounts in the deferred cash-flow profile. Thus, it turns out that clever manipulation of an arithmetic gradient series cash flow can create unfounded perceptions of the worth of a professional sports contract. This may explain why some sports professionals end up almost bankrupt even after receiving what they assume to be multi-million-dollar contracts. Similar examples have been found in reviewing the contracts of other sports professionals.

Chapter 11

Geometric Series Cash Flow

In an increasing geometric series cash flow, the amounts in the cash flow increase by a constant percentage from period to period. There is a positive base amount, A_1, at the end of period one as shown in the figure below.

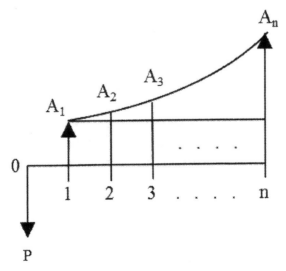

The amount at time t is calculated as a percentage of the amount at the preceding period. That is,

$$A_t = A_{t-1}(1+j), \text{ for } t = 1, 2, 3, \ldots, n$$

In the above, j is the percentage increase in the cash flow from one period to the next period. If j is negative, the geometric series will be decreasing instead of increasing. The general formula for A_t is shown below.

$$A_t = A_1(1+j)^{t-1}, \text{ for } t=1, 2, 3, \ldots, n$$

A_1 is the first amount (at time 1) in the cash flow series. The formula for calculating the present worth of the increasing geometric series cash flow is as shown below.

$$P = A_1[1 - (1+j)^n(1+i)^{-n}]/(i-j)$$

If $i = j$, the formula above reduces to the expression below.

$$P = nA_1/(1+i), \text{ when } i=j$$

Example

Suppose funding for a five-year project is to increase by 6% every year, with an initial funding of \$20,000 at the end of the first year. Determine how much must be deposited into a budget account at time zero in order to cover the anticipated funding levels if the budget account pays 10% interest per year. We have $j = 6\%$, $i = 10\%$, $n = 5$, $A_1 = \$20,000$. Therefore,

$$P = 20,000[1 - (1+0.06)^5(1+0.10)^{-5}]/(0.10 - 0.06) = \$84,533.60$$

Decreasing Geometric Series Cash Flow

In a decreasing geometric series cash flow, the amounts in the cash flow decrease by a constant percentage from period to period. The cash flow starts at some positive base amount, A_1. The applicable formulas are shown below.

$$A_t = A_{t-1}(1-j), \text{ for } t = 1, 2, 3, \ldots, n$$

$$P = A_1[1 - (1-j)^n(1+i)^{-n}]/(i+j)$$

The variable j is the percentage decrease in the cash flow from period to period.

Example

A contract amount for a three-year project is expected to decrease by 10% every year with an initial contract of $100,000 at the end of the first year. Determine how much must be available in a contract reservoir fund at time zero in order to cover the contract amounts. The fund pays 10% interest per year. Since $j = 10\%$, $i = 10\%$, $n = 3$, $A_1 = \$100,000$, we should have the following result.

$$P = 100,000[1+(1+0.10)^3(1+0.10)^{-3}]/(0.10+0.10) = \$226,150.00$$

Chapter 12

Benefit-Cost Ratio

Benefit/Cost (B/C) ratio analysis is a simple method of quickly assessing the economic suitability of an endeavor. It is frequently used for evaluating public projects. It has its origins in the Flood Act of 1936, which requires that for a federally financed project to be justified, its benefits must, at a minimum, equal its costs. B/C ratio is the systematic method of calculating the ratio of project benefits to project costs at a discounted rate. It provides a quick "go" or "no-go" decision. The benefit-cost ratio of a cash flow is the ratio of the present worth of benefits (incomes) to the present worth of costs (expenditures). This is defined as shown below.

$$B/C = PW_{(of\ benefits)}/PW_{(of\ costs)}$$

The PW values are calculated by the present value formulas presented earlier. If the benefit-cost ratio is greater than one, the investment is judged to be acceptable. If the ratio is less than one, the investment is not acceptable. A ratio of one indicates a break-even situation for the project.

Example

Consider the following investment opportunity by a city.

Initial Cost	= $600,000
Benefit per year at the end of Years 1 and 2	= 30,000
Benefit per year at the end of Years 3 to 30	= 50,000

If the city sets the interest rate at 7% per year, would this be an economically feasible investment?

Solution

$PW_{benefits}$ = 30,000(P/A,7%, 2) + 50,000(P/A,7%, 28)(P/F,7%, 2)
= $584,267.16

PW_{costs} = $600,000

B/C = 584,267.16/600,000
= 0.97

The B/C ratio indicates that the investment is not economically feasible since the B/C < 1.0.

Chapter 13

Payback Period

On the lighter side, payback period does not mean how much time you have left to get even with an enemy. The term "payback period" refers to the length of time it will take to recover an initial investment. The approach does not consider the impact of the time value of money. Consequently, it is not an accurate method of evaluating the worth of an investment. However, it is a simple technique used widely to perform a quick-and-dirty or superficial assessment of investment performance. The technique considers only the initial cost. Other costs that may occur after time zero are not included in the calculation. The payback period is defined as the smallest value of n (in years) that satisfies the following expression.

Payback period "PB" is the number of years at which the sum of revenues (or savings) equal or exceed the initial cost. That is,

$$R_1 + R_2 + R_3 + \ldots + R_{PB} >= C_0$$

$$\sum_{t=1}^{n_{min}} R_t \geq C$$

where R_t is the revenue at time t and C_0 is the initial cost. The procedure calls for a simple addition of the revenues period by period until enough total has been accumulated to offset the initial cost.

Example

An organization is considering installing a new computer system that will generate significant savings in material and labor requirements for order processing. The system has an initial cost of $50,000. It is expected to save the organization $20,000 a year. The system has an anticipated useful life of five years with a salvage value of $5,000. Determine how long it will take for the system to pay for itself from the savings it is expected to generate. Since the annual savings are uniform, we can calculate the payback period by simply dividing the initial cost by the annual savings. That is,

$$PB = \$50,000/\$20,000 = 2.5 \text{ years}$$

Note that the salvage value of $5,000 is not included in the above calculation since the amount is not realized until the end of the useful life of the asset (i.e., after five years). In some cases, it may be desired to consider the salvage value. In that case, the amount to be offset by the annual savings will be the net cost of the asset, represented here as shown below.

$$PB = (\$50,000 - \$5,000)/\$20,000 = 2.25 \text{ years}$$

If there are tax liabilities associated with the annual savings, those liabilities must be deducted from the savings before calculating the payback period. The simple payback period does not take the time value of money into consideration. It is, however, a concept readily understood by people unfamiliar with economic analysis.

Discounted Payback Period

The discounted payback period is a payback analysis approach in which the revenues are reinvested at a certain interest rate. The payback period is determined when enough money has been accumulated at the given interest rate to offset the initial cost as well as other interim costs. In this case, the calculation is done by summing up the series of future values generated by the revenues. It is best done through a cumulative tabulation approach.

Example

A new solar panel system is to be installed in an office complex at an initial cost of $150,000. It is expected that the system will generate annual cost savings of $22,500 on the electricity bill. The solar system will need to be overhauled every five years at a cost of $5,000 per overhaul. If the annual interest rate is 10%, find the discounted payback period for the system considering the time value of money. The costs of overhaul are to be considered in calculating the discounted payback period.

Solution

Using the single payment compound amount factor for one period iteratively, the cumulative solution below is obtained.

Time 1: $22,500
Time 2: $22,500 + $22,500 $(1.10)^1$ = $47,250
Time 3: $22,500 + $47,250 $(1.10)^1$ = $74,475
Time 4: $22,500 + $74,475 $(1.10)^1$ = $104,422.50
Time 5: $22,500 + $104,422.50 $(1.10)^1$ - $5000 = $132,364.75
Time 6: $22,500 + $132,364.75 $(1.10)^1$ = $168,101.23

The initial investment is $150,000. By the end of period 6, we have accumulated $168,101.23, which is more than the initial cost. So, the payback period is set at 6 years. That is, it will take six years for the solar panel system to pay for itself.

Chapter 14

Fixed and Variable Interest Rates

An interest rate may be fixed or may vary from period to period over the useful life of an investment. Some of the factors responsible for varying interest rates include changes in nominal and international economies, effects of inflation, and changes in the market. Loan rates, such as mortgage loan rates, may be adjusted from year to year based on the inflation index of the Consumer Price Index (CPI). If the variations in interest rate from period to period are not large, cash-flow calculations usually ignore their effects. However, the results of the computation will vary considerably if the variations in interest rates are large. In such cases, the varying interest rates should be considered in economic analysis, even though such consideration may become computationally involved.

Example

Find the present worth of the following cash flows if for n < 5, i = 0.5% and for n > 4, i = 0.25%.

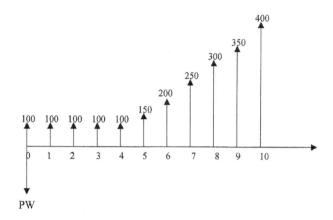

PW

Solution

This is typical of several real-world cash flows. The computation must be done carefully.
Using the present worth formulas presented earlier, the calculation is done as shown below.

$$
\begin{aligned}
P \quad &= 100 + 100(P/A, 0.5\%, 4) + [150(P/A, 0.25\%, 6) \\
&\quad + 50\ (P/G, 0.25\%, 6)](P/F, 0.5\%, 4) \\
&= 100+100(3.950)+[150(5.948)+50(14.826)](0.9802) \\
&= \$2{,}096.16
\end{aligned}
$$

Therefore, the present value for these cash flows with two different interest rates is $2,096.16. The interest rate for n > 4 affects only cash flows in periods 5 to 10, whereas the interest rate for n < 5 affects cash flows in periods 1 to 10.

Dangers of Variable Interest Rates

One danger is using variable interest rate is that the consumer does not know what the future holds. A stable interest rate today may not be stable tomorrow. An interest rate that is projected to be stable in the future may, indeed, become erratic. In spite of promises made by the lender, a future interest rate that is pegged at a certain level may become adjustable to the detriment of the borrower. Lenders have well-practiced means of finagling future terms to come out in their favor. If the consumer thinks that the lender is legally bound to abide by the promise in the signed document, what happens when the lender suddenly sells the loan to another lender, whose loans are on different terms?

Loan Shark Caution

Not only do variable interest rates portend hidden dangers, they also suggest caution about other types of interest rate manipulations. *Loan Sharks*, now popular known as payday lenders, can manipulate interest rates for their own business advantage to the detriment of the borrower. In the heydays of rampant loan sharking, interest rates were often quoted in small fragmented increments. For example, a quote of 1% per week over the loan period may, on the surface, appear to be a bargain considering only the absolute magnitude of the quoted rate. An untrained consumer mind might jump at the offer of "1%" without factoring in the effective annual rate implications. After all, "1%" sounds more attractive than whatever can be obtained at any friendly neighborhood bank. But, the actual annual impact on the borrower's pocket means a nominal interest rate of 1% per week for 52 weeks per year. That is, a nominal annual interest rate of 52%. Would you borrow money at 52% if it is quoted to you in this format? I didn't think so. The loan shark knows that. So, he or she quotes only the weekly rate, which, psychologically, appears to be quite acceptable.

Now, there is more. If that rate of 1% per week is compounded on a daily basis, which is the way an unscrupulous lender might operate, then the annual effective impact is even worse. If compounded on a daily basis, a 1% rate per week will translate to an effective annual rate of 68.38%. Only desperately hopeless borrowers will succumb to such an exorbitant rate. If the 1% per week interest rate is compounded on a weekly basis, then the effective annual rate will be 67.77%. This is lower than the daily compounding rate, but hardly any relief is achieved. As mentioned earlier, the more frequently the interest rate is compounded, the higher the effective annual rate, and the more the adverse impact on the borrower's pocket. The key to making the right decision about loan rate offers is to ask questions and to get alternate opinions from independent financial analysts, if the computational analysis cannot be done directly by the borrower himself or herself.

Chapter 15

Mortgage Loan Analysis

Owning a home and having a mortgage loan constitute a part of the "American Dream." Without an ability to accumulate enough cash up front, most homeowners must resort to mortgage loans as a vehicle for raising sufficient money to buy their homes. The typical length of a mortgage loan is 30 years. This is a long, long time to hold a loan. The longer the life of the loan, the higher the interest charges that the borrower pays the lender. Mortgage lending offers a good demonstration of the time value of money. The long cycle time of mortgage loans provides a basis for jokes about the impact of mortgages. One popular quote says,

> "Mortgages are the best way to get people
> thinking about the afterlife."

This may not be too far-fetched when we consider a French interpretation of mortgage.

"Mort" in French means "death."
"Gage" in French means "pledge."
So, "mortgage" implies "death pledge."

Scary! But it could be rational if you consider that a 65-year-old person getting a 30-year mortgage will be paying on the mortgage until age 95. So, "mortgage" metaphorically signifies the burden of mortgage loans.

It is quite revealing (and may be depressing) to find out how much of your mortgage payments go into interest charges the longer you hold the loan. For this reason, 10-year and 15-year mortgages have become attractive to those who can afford the higher monthly interest payments.

In the early days of desktop computers in the mid-1980s, prior to the prevalence of the Internet, this author developed the first share computer program to do mortgage payments analysis*. The program, called GAMPS, later became the fore-runner of other software offerings as well as commercial software tools for mortgage payments analysis.

----

*Reference:
Badiru, A. B., "Graphical Analysis of Mortgage Payments," Proceedings of 8th Annual Conference on Computers and Industrial Engineering, Orlando, Florida, March 1986, Computers and Industrial Engineering, Vol. 11, Nos. 1-4, 1986, pp. 421-425.

Nowadays, there are a slew of software tools available through the Internet for mortgage analysis. They all use the same basic principles, formulas, and computational techniques presented in this book.

For calculation purposes in this book, we will use the following notations.

U_t = unpaid balance immediately after making payment number t

A = installment payment per period

E_t = amount of principal in payment t = equity payment

I_t = amount of interest in payment number t

The mortgage cash flow profiles looks like a typical uniform series compound amount cash flow as presented in the preceding chapters. Two examples are shown below. In the second diagram, the unpaid balance at time t is shown. The unpaid balance is the present worth (at time t) for the future monthly payments that are yet to be paid.

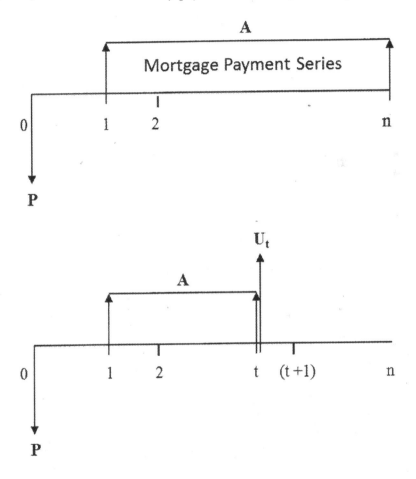

The computational procedure for analyzing the mortgage cash flow follows the steps outlined below.

1. Given a principal amount, P, a periodic interest rate, i (in decimals), and a discrete time span of n periods, the uniform series of equal end-of-period payments needed to amortize P is computed as

$$A = \frac{P\left[i(1+i)^n\right]}{(1+i)\ -1}.$$

It is assumed that the loan is to be repaid in equal monthly payments. Thus, $A(t) = A$, for each period t throughout the life of the loan.

2. The unpaid balance after making t installment payments is given by

$$U(t) = \frac{A\left[1-(1+i)^{(t-n)}\right]}{i}.$$

Using the interest tables, U_t = A(P/A, i%, n-t)

3. The amount of equity or principal amount paid with installment payment number t is given by

$$E(t) = A(1+i)^{t-n-1}.$$

Using the interest tables, E_t = A(P/F, i%, n-t+1).

4. The amount of interest charge contained in installment payment number t is derived to be

$$I(t) = A\left[1-(1+i)^{t-n-1}\right].$$

Using the interest tables, I_t = A[1 − (P/F, i%, n-t+1)].
Note that $A = E(t) + I(t)$. That is, each payment consists of equity and interest payment.

5. The cumulative total payment made after t periods is denoted by

$$C(t) = (A)(t).$$

6. The cumulative interest payment after t periods is given by

$$Q(t) = \sum_{x=1}^{t} I(x).$$

7. The cumulative principal payment after t periods is computed as

$$S(t) = A\left[\frac{(1+i)^t - 1}{i(1+i)^n}\right]$$

8. The percentage of interest charge contained in installment payment number t is

$$p(t) = \frac{I(t)}{A}(100\%).$$

9. The percentage of cumulative interest charge contained in the cumulative total payment up to and including payment number t is

$$P(t) = \frac{Q(t)}{C(t)}(100\%).$$

10. The percentage of cumulative principal payment contained in the cumulative total payment up to and including payment number t is

$$H(t) = \frac{S(t)}{C(t)}(100\%).$$

Example

Consider the case of a consumer who bought a $130,000 house with a down payment of $30,000. The balance of $100,000 is financed over 25 years at an interest rate of 12% per year compounded monthly. That is, i = 1% per month. Do a mortgage analysis of this mortgage scenario. What is the unpaid balance after five years?

Solution

25 years = 300 months
i = 1% per month
Monthly payment = A = $100,000 (A/P, 1%, 300) = $1,053/month
After 5 years (60 months), the mortgage cash flow looks as shown in the figure below.

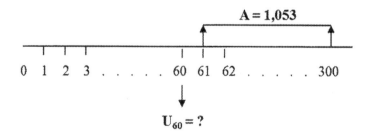

Using the unpaid balance formula presented earlier, the unpaid balance for this mortgage transaction at time t=60 is calculated as follows.

U_{60} = $1,053(P/A, 1%, 300-60) = $1,053(P/A, 1%, 240) = $95,633

Equity after 5 years is the total amount of principal amounts paid over the five years. This is calculated as the initial principal amount minus the unpaid balance at the five-year point. That is,

Equity = $100,000 - $95,633 = $4,367.

Now, the total payment made over 5 years = $1,053(60) = $63,180.

Therefore, the total interest paid after 5 years is the total payments made minus the cumulative equity. That is,

Interest Paid = $63,180 - $4367 = $58,813.

Thus, the percentage of the total payment going into interest charges is calculated as shown below.

Interest Percentage = ($58,813/$63,180)100% = 93.1%.

The mortgage formulas are applicable to any loan amortization schedule, not just mortgage loans.

Example

Suppose a manufacturing productivity improvement project is to be financed by borrowing $500,000 from an industrial development bank. The annual nominal interest rate for the loan is 10%. The loan is to be repaid in equal monthly installments over a period of 15 years. The first payment on the loan is to be made exactly one month after financing is approved. A detailed analysis of the loan schedule is desired.

Solution

The calculation approach presented above shows a monthly payment of $5,373.03 on the loan. As an illustration, at time $t = 10$ months, we have the following calculations.

$U(10)$ = $487,473.83 (unpaid balance)
$A(10)$ = $5,373.03 (monthly payment)
$E(10)$ = $1,299.91 (equity portion of the tenth payment)
$I(10)$ = $4,073.11 (interest charge contained in the tenth payment)
$C(10)$ = $53,730.26 (total payment to date)

$S(10) = \$12,526.17$ (total equity to date)

$p(10) = 75.81\%$ (percentage of the tenth payment going into interest charge)

$P(10) = 76.69\%$ (percentage of the total payment going into interest charge over the first 10 months).

Over 76% of the sum of the first ten installment payments goes into interest charges. The analysis shows that by time $t = 180$, the unpaid balance has been reduced to zero. That is, $U(180) = 0.0$. The total payment made on the loan is $967,144.61 and the total interest charge is $967,144.61 - $500,000 = $467,144.61. So, 48.30% of the total payment goes into interest charges. The information about interest charges might be very useful for tax purposes. The full calculations for this example show that equity builds up slowly and the unpaid balance decreases slowly. Very little equity is accumulated during the first three years of the loan schedule. The effects of inflation, depreciation, property appreciation, and other economic factors are not included in the analysis presented above, but a project analysis should include such factors whenever they are relevant to an actual loan situation. Some interesting graphical plots for this example are shown below.

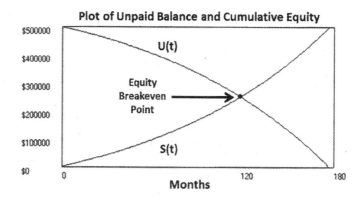

The figure below shows a plot of the total loan payment and the cumulative equity with respect to time. The total payment starts from $0.0 at time 0 and goes up to $967,144.61 by the end of the last month of the installment payments. Since only $500,000 was borrowed, the total interest payment on the loan is $967,144.61 - $500,000 = $467,144.61.

The cumulative principal payment starts at $0.0 at time 0 and slowly builds up to $500,000.00, which is the original loan amount.

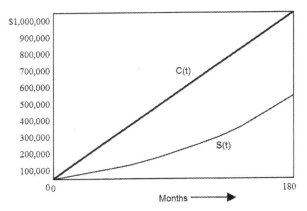

The figure below presents a plot of the percentage of interest charge in the monthly payments and the percentage of interest charge in the total payment. The percentage of interest charge in the monthly payments starts at 77.55% for the first month and decreases to 0.83% for the last month. By comparison, the percentage of interest in the total payment starts also at 77.55% for the first month and slowly decreases to 48.30% by the time the last payment is made at time 180. An increasing proportion of the monthly payment goes into the principal payment as time goes on. If the interest charges are tax-deductible, the decreasing values of $f(t)$ mean that there would be decreasing tax benefits from the interest charges in the later months of the loan.

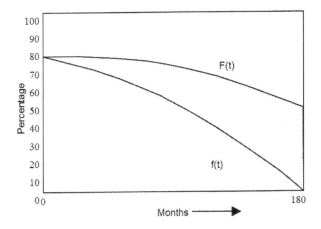

Balloon Payment Danger

A balloon payment is a single payment to retire a loan at the end of the loan duration. While this option gives the borrower relief from having to deal with interim periodic payments, it does have a huge downside. The danger of a balloon payment is the enormous size of the single future payment. Consider the example above, where the principal loan amount is $500,000 and the interest rate is 10% for a 15-year term. If this was to be paid by one balloon payment, the amount will be calculated as shown below.

P = $500,000
i = 10% per year compounded per year = 0.833333% per month
n = 15 years = 180 months

Using the single payment compound amount factor formula, the single balloon payment at the end of 180 months is calculated as shown below.

$$F_{180} = \$500,000 \ (1 + 0.00833333)^{180} = \$500,000 \ (4.453919287)$$
$$= \$2,226,959.64$$

This is a huge amount that the borrower must come up with suddenly at the end of the loan. A comparison of the two repayment approaches is tabulated below.

Loan Attribute	Amortization Payment	Balloon Payment
Loan amount	$500,000	$500,000
Loan life	15 years	15 years
Interest rate	10% per year	10% per year
Total Repayment	$967,144.61	$2,226,959.64
Total Interest	$467,144.61	$1,726,959.64

You be the judge. Which one of the two options is in the interest (pun intended) of the borrower?

If the balloon payment is calculated using the interest rate table, the format will be written as follows.

$$F_{180} = \$500,000(F/P, 0.83333\%, 180) = \$2,226,959.78$$

This yielded the same result as we obtained by using the formula approach. Round-off errors and differences can occur in the calculations depending on how many decimals places are used in the formula calculations and the size of the base amount. A good rule of thumb is to use 10 decimal places or take the decimal places to as many as your calculator can handle. This author has served as an expert witness in a financial transaction lawsuit where the bone of contention was whether a lender knowingly manipulated decimal places calculations to the detriment of the borrower. If your interest table does not have the actual interest rate you are dealing with, then you must use the formulas for your calculations. Just remember to convert the interest rate percentage to decimals before plugging into the formulas.

Chapter 16

Equity Break-Even Point

In the mortgage analysis presented in the preceding chapter, the point at which the unpaid balance curve and the cumulative equity curve intersect is derived by this author and called the *equity break-even point*. It indicates when the unpaid balance is exactly equal to the accumulated equity or the cumulative principal payment. For the preceding example, the equity break-even point is approximately 120 months (10 years). The importance of the equity break-even point is that any equity accumulated after that point represents the amount of ownership or equity that the debtor is entitled to after the unpaid balance on the loan is settled with the project collateral. The implication of this is very important, particularly in the case of mortgage loans. The equity break-even point can be calculated directly from the formula derived below.

Let the equity break-even point, x, be defined as the point where $U(t) = S(t)$. That is,

$$A\left[\frac{1-(1+i)^{-(n-t)}}{i}\right] = A\left[\frac{(1+i)^t - 1}{i(1+i)^n}\right].$$

After much algebraic manipulation, the above expression reduces to the following formula.

$$t_{ebp} = \frac{\ln\left[0.5(1+i)^n + 0.5\right]}{\ln(1+i)}$$

ln is the natural log function,
n is the number of periods in the life of the loan, and
i is the interest rate per period in decimals.

Example

Suppose a 30-year mortgage loan of $320,000 is financed at annual interest rate of 3.45%. What is the equity breakeven point for this mortgage?

Solution

From the data given, n = 12(30) = 360 months, P = 320,000, i = 3.45% per year compounded per year compounded per month. Thus, the interest rate per month is 3.45%/12 = 0.2875% per month = 0.002875.

x = {ln[0.5(1.002875)^{360} + 0.5]}/ln(1.002875) = **18.72 years**

The stage-by-stage calculations are shown below.

x   = {ln[0.5(2.8109289981) + 0.5]}/0.0028708750917
        = {ln[1.9054644]}/0.0028708750917
        = 0.6447257584/0.0028708750917
        = 224.58 months
        = 18.72 years

In another case example (details not shown here), the equity breakeven point for a 30-year loan is calculated to 28.95 years. Yikes! This is quite revealing (and may be depressing) to know. The higher the interest rate and the longer the life of the loan, the farther away is the equity breakeven point. Knowing these numbers in advance may prompt the consumer to negotiate or shop around for better mortgage rates and terms. In fact, experimenting with different scenario computations up front may guide the consumer before actually approaching and discussing with prospective lenders.

Chapter 17

Accelerated Mortgage Payoff

The time value of money implies that you pay more interest charges the longer you keep a loan. So, the goal of the consumer should be to keep a loan as short as possible. That is, the quicker you pay off a loan, the lower your overall interest charges.

Many homeowners often receive advertisement in the mail offering accelerated mortgage payoff terms. Such offers must be evaluated carefully to sort out any hidden dangers. Even if the calculations are correct, the goal of the lender may be to get a borrower to switch from his or her existing "friendly neighborhood" lender. One common advertisement is echoed in the example tabulated below.

Commercial Advertisement Sample

Bi-weekly Payment Option: Half of regular monthly payment
For example, if monthly payments are $1,000 each, then the bi-weekly payment will be $500.

Loan Attributes (Quoted)	Regular Option	Bi-weekly Option
Loan Term	30 years	23.9 years
Loan Term Reduction	0 years	6.1 years
Approximate Interest Savings	$0	$52,440
Monthly Interest Savings	$0	$183.36

The fine print says the following. "Sample figures only: $276,000, 30-year fixed term, $2,058 monthly payment includes average escrow, savings is net of all fees based on bi-weekly program for life of the loan, sample 5.0 interest rate (not your actual rate) used to calculate savings."

Analysis of the Sample

For one thing, the word "Approximate" is a loaded terminology giving the lender a way out should a contention develop about the actual numbers later on. Remember that finagling the terms and decimal places in the calculations can cause changes. Minute changes may not matter much to the borrower. But for the lender, the sum of all those small changes over a large number of borrowers can translate to a huge profit. This is why lenders want more borrowers, even if the case of a single borrower does not amount to much.

Also, notice the sample interest rate is quoted as 5%. If the current market rates are lower than that, using the higher interest rate for the sample will produce magnitudes of savings higher than what the consumer will actually experience at the going market interest rate. To analyze the viability of this offer, the consumer should use the current market-level interest rate.

Further, the monthly interest savings quoted as $183.36 is misleading. As we have seen in the preceding calculations of mortgage analysis, the interest charge contained in each monthly payment decreases over time. So, quoting a single amount, (perhaps the very first one) sends a misleading message that the same high value will be saved every month throughout the life of the loan. This is, certainly, not true.

Computational Verification

If we do the calculations for the numbers provided in the sample, below is what we will find.

Loan amount: $276,000
Term: 30 years (360 months)
Interest rate = 5% per year compounded per month.
i = 5%/12 = 0.41667% per month

Calculation of Regular Monthly Payment:
A = $276,000 (A/P, 0.41667%, 360) = $1,481.63 per month
This does not agree with the $2,058 per month quoted in the fine print above. So, something else may be missing in the data given. Of course, the assumptions stated about escrow and fees include some hidden numbers not revealed in this advertisement example. So, the moral here is "Buyer Beware!"

Since 0.41667% does not appear in any interest tables, the above was calculated using the single payment capital recovery formula.

Now, if the original monthly cash flow is converted to a bi-weekly cash flow, we will have 2x360 = 720 payments (i.e., 720 bi-weekly periods). If this is done properly, the interest rate of 5% must be compounded bi-weekly. Thus, the calculation interest rate will be 5%/24 = 0.208333% per bi-weekly because there are 24 bi-weekly in each year.
If half of the regular monthly payment is made each bi-weekly, that amount will be $1,481.63/2 = $740.82 per bi-weekly (fortnight).

Subsequent calculations must then be made with the following variables.

A = $740.82 per fortnight
i = 0.208333% per fortnight
n = 720 fortnights
Fortnight (a British term) is used interchangeable for bi-weekly in the discussions here.

Now, to verify the 6.1 years quoted in the loan term reduction, we will have to find the value of n (in fortnights) needed to retire the loan of $276,000 by paying $740.82 every two weeks at the interest rate of 0.208333% per fortnight. The setup appears as follows.

$$\$276,000 = \$740.82 \ (P/A, \ 0.208333\%, \ n)$$
or
$$\$740.82 = \$276,000 \ (A/P, \ 0.208333\%, \ n)$$

The goal is to find a value of n that makes the above equations true.

In the uniform series present worth formula setup, we have the following.

$$\$276,000 = \$740.82 \ [(1.00208333)^n - 1]/[(0.00208333)(1.00208333)^n]$$
or
$$[(1.00208333)^n - 1]/[(0.00208333)(1.00208333)^n] = 372.56$$

It is no trivial matter to solve for the value of n in the above equation. Many times, it is done by trial-and-error of various n values as well as algebraic interpolation. This is well above the computational capability of an ordinary consumer and the lenders know it. A spreadsheet calculation method can help the consumer to experiment with possible values of n that satisfy the equation.

After much finagling (details not shown here), the value of n is found to be 720 fortnights, which agrees perfectly with the term that we started with. So, where does the reduction in the loan life come from? As mentioned earlier, escrow and fees may mask the actual figures applicable to an exact calculation to verify this example.

So, now, let's use the $2,058 per month quoted in the advertisement to do our verification calculations. Obviously, this is where the escrow and fees are embedded. In this case, the bi-weekly payments are $2,058/2 = $1,029 per fortnight.

Repeating the verification calculations with this alternate number, we have the following.

$$\$276,000 = \$1,029\ [(1.00208333)^n - 1]/[(0.00208333)(1.00208333)^n]$$
or
$$[(1.00208333)^n - 1]/[(0.00208333)(1.00208333)^n] = 268.22$$

Using Microsoft Excel trial-and-error calculations, the value of n that satisfies the above equation comes out to be 394 fortnights, which is 197 months, which is 16.42 years.

This means that if you religiously make payments of $2,058 per month, the loan amount of $276,000 should be retired in 16.42 years, a savings of 13.58 years (i.e., 30 -16.42 = 13.58). Since the offer is quoting a savings of only 6.1 years, it means there are some other aspects of this offer that are not clear in the advertisement. In other words, we don't have all the numbers, terms, and nuances. So, it is difficult to verify the actual savings based on what is provided in the advertisement. This does not mean that the lender is doing anything wrong. We should note, once again, that there are legal ways to manipulate cash flows and interest rates to create one perception or another in the mind of the consumer. Common examples can be found in professional sports contracts as mentioned earlier in the case of Steve Young of the LA Express in 1984. Case examples with coaching contracts abound in the Press. In his days of teaching engineering economic analysis, this author used several pro sports contract cash flows as classroom examples to illustrate how cash flow calculations are done. The author was teaching at the University of Tennessee when the contract details for Bruce Pearl, the basketball coach, were publicly released (http://www.utsports.com/sports/m-baskbl/spec-rel/030806aac.html).
Extracting additional details about the contract, the author compiled the following cash flow arrangement.

2007-2008: Total Compensation -- $1.3 Million
2008-2009: Total Compensation -- $1.4 Million
2009-2010: Total Compensation -- $1.5 Million
2010-201: Total Compensation -- $1.6 Million
2011-2012: Total Compensation -- $1.7 Million
2012-2013: Total Compensation -- $1.8 Million

This is, obviously, an arithmetic gradient series cash flow, which is discussed in previous chapters. Recall that gradient cash flows can be used to manipulate the raw appearances of the present value of a contract. For the Bruce Pearl contract, the following calculations are done.

Given Data

Constant amount **A=$1.1million** according to Volunteer TV
Constant average amount of **$1.3 million** according to CSTV
Time = n = 6 years (2006/2007 to 2011/2012)
Base salary = $300,000
TV and radio appearances =$300,000
Endorsements = $ $300,000
Public Relations =$150,000
Sports Camp =$50,000
Assumption: Interest rate =10% per year

From Total of Volunteer TV data:

$$PW_{total} = A(P/A, i\%, n) = \$1.1\text{million } (P|A, 10\%, 6)$$
$$= 1,100,000 \ (4.3553) = \$4,790,830$$

From CSTV Average:

$$PW_{total} = A(P/A, i\%, n) = \$1.3\text{million } (P|A, 10\%, 6)$$
$$= 1,300,000 \ (4.3553) = \$5,661,890$$

The Buyout

Buyout payment = $1million over 3 years.
Assumption: He pays constant amount per month for 36 months at the interest rate of10% per year (i.e., 0.8333% per month)
A=$27,778 per month.

Using the above assumptions we calculate the present worth of his buyout:

$$PW_{buyout} = A(P/A, i\%, n) = \$27,778 \ (P|A, 10\%, 36)$$
$$= \$27,778 \ (31.00) = \$861,118.00$$

Therefore, the present worth of the buyout is \$861,118. As can be seen from the above calculations, if the time value of money is considered, cash flows can reveal more than the ordinary consumer perceives the cash flow to be. For this reason, a professional athlete can easily and quickly get in financial trouble if he spends much more money upfront (on cars, houses, big-ticket items, etc.) than the present value of his contract. Newspaper columnist, Jerry Greene, in his 1984 column in the Orlando News Sentinel, opined that "an athlete needs not only an agent to watch what the club is doing, but also an attorney to watch what the agent is doing." This author would add the need for a financial analyst to watch how all the cash flow transactions are configured.

Chapter 18

Rule of 72

A topic that is often of intense interest in many investment scenarios is how long it will take a given amount to reach a certain multiple of its initial level. The "Rule of 72" is one simple approach to calculating how long it will take an investment to double in value at a given interest rate per period. The Rule of 72 gives the following formula for estimating the doubling period.

$$n = 72/i$$

The interest rate, i, is expressed in percentage. This formula estimates the future value of an investment as double the initial value. That is, $F = 2P$.

Example

Suppose an amount of $25,000 is invested in an account that pays 5.25% per year. How long will it take for the account to double in value?

Solution

$$n = 72/5.25 = 13.71 \text{ years.}$$

This is a simple and quick way to assess the future worth of simple investments, if there are no financial disruptions.

Chapter 19

Tips for Consumer Economics

1. Time value of money is the key to realizing a healthy future worth.
2. Based on the time value of money, no amount of money is too small to invest. A small amount invested over a long period of time can amount to a fortune. Discipline and fortitude are needed to leave the investment alone, except in the case of catastrophic emergency needs.
3. It takes money to earn money. You must be willing to spend (i.e., invest) in order to have a chance to earn money from your money.
4. Risk comes with every investment opportunity. Don't shun risk, manage it and move forward. Like a saying goes, "In order to accumulate, you must speculate."
5. Whether you are risk averse or risk seeking, time is on your side for time value of money.
6. Depending on your personal level of risk averseness, diversify your investments. Safe and stable investment options may earn little in the short term, but they accumulate value over time.
7. Put your money away for the long haul.
8. Don't starve and deprive yourself for the sake of putting money away. You can always spend interest incomes on yourself as long as you let the base amount do its work.
9. You don't have to have a fortune to leverage the power of compound interest and the time value of money. Small amounts put away

regularly and religiously can accumulate a substantial amount of money in the long haul.

10. Stay the course. Remain dedicated to the personal mission of watching your money.

Chapter 20

Examples to Ponder

At this point, readers who have gotten this far, learned a lot, and may be interested in a personal challenge of understanding have an opportunity here to ponder a few examples on their own. Some of the details in the examples are fictitious to protect both the innocent and the guilty. However, the numbers are representative of typical scenarios in consumer economics.

Example 1

It was recently reported (in the Newspapers) that a club has signed a basketball star for a deal worth $13.8 million. The details of the contract are:

$4 million as a signing bonus to be paid now
$3 million salary for Year 1
$2.2 million salary for Year 2
$2.4 million salary for Year 3
$2.2 million salary for Year 4

Each annual salary is to be paid in 12 equal end-of-month payments. The monthly salary is calculated as the annual salary divided by 12. Find the present worth of this Sports contract if annual interest rate is 12%. Compare the reported contract value of $13.8 million to the actual present worth of the contract. What is your impression of the newspaper report?

Example 2

The City of Newcity has decided to sell 20-year bonds to raise funds to attract a new engineering company to the city. The total face value of the bonds is $5,000,000 and the annual bond rate is 9% payable quarterly. At the time of the purchase, the bond buyers will pay a processing fee which is 2% of the bond price. If the effective annual interest rate is 15%, what is the maximum fair price that buyers should pay for the bonds?

Example 3

An engineer financed a house for $100,000 and he is paying for it over a period of 30 years through monthly payments. The annual interest rate is 12%.

a) What percentage of his total dollar payments in the first year goes into interest payments?
b) If he wants to pay off the loan at the beginning of the sixth year, how much lump sum would be required?

Example 4

To make his cash flow stronger, an author used the quarterly dollar cash flow design below.

a) Find the future value of the cash flow at time t = 20 if the nominal interest rate is 24% per year.

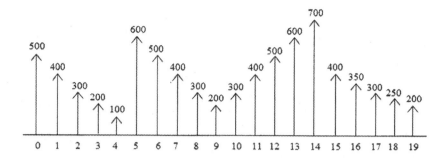

b) Suppose the author decides to use the future worth in Part (a) above to establish a scholarship endowment for engineering so that scholarships can be awarded to the best students each and every year forever. For the purpose of setting up the endowment, a friendly neighborhood bank has offered to compound the annual interest rate of 12% on a monthly basis. Find the amount of annual scholarship that will be awarded from this endowment.

Example 4

Using the calculation procedures presented for the accelerated mortgage payoff example, find the accelerated payoff years for a 30-year loan of $100,000 with an interest rate of 12% per year if the original monthly payment is to be made bi-weekly. That is, half of the monthly payment is paid every two weeks. Assuming no other data is available, how many years is saved on the 30-year term by going to a bi-weekly schedule?

Conclusion

The examples presented above are for the purpose of encouraging the reader to test his or her own mastery of the contents presented in this book. Readers are encouraged to seek other personal examples where the applications of economic analysis can be practiced. The tables in the Appendix cover only a limited collection of typical interest rate tables. For readers' applications outside the selected interest rates in the appendix, the general formulas provided in the book may be used. I hope that this brief journey through *Consumer Economics* has created an increased interest in the time value of money and the power of compound interest. I wish every reader a happy and successful application of the concepts, tools, models, and techniques presented in this book.

About the author

Deji Badiru is an award-winning author, educator, researcher, and administrator. He is a registered professional engineer, a Fellow of the Institute of Industrial Engineers, and a Fellow of the Nigerian Academy of Engineering. He holds a B.S. in industrial engineering, an M.S. in mathematics, an M.S. in industrial engineering from Tennessee Technological University, and a Ph.D. in industrial engineering from the University of Central Florida. Badiru also holds a leadership certificate from the University of Tennessee. He is a member of several professional organizations and author of several books and technical journal articles. He has served as a consultant to several organizations around the world and has received awards for his teaching, writing, and leading teams. Badiru has diverse areas of avocation. His professional accomplishments are coupled with his passion for writing about everyday events, interpersonal issues, and social observations.

Appendix

Common Interest Rate Formulas and Tables

Name of Factor	Formula	Table Notation
Compound Amount (single payment)	$(1+i)^N$	(F/P, i, N)
Present Worth (single payment)	$(1+i)^{-N}$	(P/F, i, N)
Sinking Fund	$\dfrac{i}{(1+i)^N - 1}$	(A/F, i, N)
Capital Recovery	$\dfrac{i(1+i)^N}{(1+i)^N - 1}$	(A/P, i, N)
Compound Amount (uniform series)	$\dfrac{(1+i)^N - 1}{i}$	(F/A, i, N)

Present Worth (uniform series)	$\dfrac{(1+i)^N - 1}{i(1+i)^N}$	(P/A, i, N)
Arithmetic Gradient to Uniform Series	$\dfrac{(1+i)^N - N - 1}{i(1+i)^N - i}$	(A/G, i, N)
Arithmetic Gradient to Present Worth	$\dfrac{(1+i)^N - N - 1}{i^2(1+i)^N}$	(P/G, i, N)
Geometric Gradient to Present Worth (for i≠g)	$\dfrac{1-(1+g)^N(1+i)^{-N}}{i-g}$	(P/A, g, i, N)

N = Number of interest periods
i = Interest rate per interest period
g = Geometric gradient cash flow growth rate

0.25%

	Single Payment		Uniform Payment Series			
	Compound Amount Factor	Present Value Factor	Sinking Fund Factor	Capital Recovery Factor	Compound Amount Factor	Present Value Factor
	Find F	Find P	Find A	Find A	Find F	Find P
Period	Given P	Given F	Given F	Given P	Given A	Given A
n	F/P	P/F	A/F	A/P	F/A	P/A
1	1.003	0.9975	1.0000	1.0025	1.000	0.998
2	1.005	0.9950	0.4994	0.5019	2.002	1.993
3	1.008	0.9925	0.3325	0.3350	3.008	2.985
4	1.010	0.9901	0.2491	0.2516	4.015	3.975
5	1.013	0.9876	0.1990	0.2015	5.025	4.963
6	1.015	0.9851	0.1656	0.1681	6.038	5.948
7	1.018	0.9827	0.1418	0.1443	7.053	6.931
8	1.020	0.9802	0.1239	0.1264	8.070	7.911
9	1.023	0.9778	0.1100	0.1125	9.091	8.889
10	1.025	0.9753	0.0989	0.1014	10.113	9.864
11	1.028	0.9729	0.0898	0.0923	11.139	10.837
12	1.030	0.9705	0.0822	0.0847	12.166	11.807
13	1.033	0.9681	0.0758	0.0783	13.197	12.775
14	1.036	0.9656	0.0703	0.0728	14.230	13.741
15	1.038	0.9632	0.0655	0.0680	15.265	14.704
16	1.041	0.9608	0.0613	0.0638	16.304	15.665
17	1.043	0.9584	0.0577	0.0602	17.344	16.623
18	1.046	0.9561	0.0544	0.0569	18.388	17.580
19	1.049	0.9537	0.0515	0.0540	19.434	18.533
20	1.051	0.9513	0.0488	0.0513	20.482	19.484
21	1.054	0.9489	0.0464	0.0489	21.533	20.433
22	1.056	0.9466	0.0443	0.0468	22.587	21.380
23	1.059	0.9442	0.0423	0.0448	23.644	22.324
24	1.062	0.9418	0.0405	0.0430	24.703	23.266
25	1.064	0.9395	0.0388	0.0413	25.765	24.205
26	1.067	0.9371	0.0373	0.0398	26.829	25.143
27	1.070	0.9348	0.0358	0.0383	27.896	26.077
28	1.072	0.9325	0.0345	0.0370	28.966	27.010
29	1.075	0.9301	0.0333	0.0358	30.038	27.940
30	1.078	0.9278	0.0321	0.0346	31.113	28.868
31	1.080	0.9255	0.0311	0.0336	32.191	29.793
32	1.083	0.9232	0.0301	0.0326	33.272	30.717
33	1.086	0.9209	0.0291	0.0316	34.355	31.638
34	1.089	0.9186	0.0282	0.0307	35.441	32.556
35	1.091	0.9163	0.0274	0.0299	36.529	33.472
36	1.094	0.9140	0.0266	0.0291	37.621	34.386
37	1.097	0.9118	0.0258	0.0283	38.715	35.298
38	1.100	0.9095	0.0251	0.0276	39.811	36.208
39	1.102	0.9072	0.0244	0.0269	40.911	37.115
40	1.105	0.9050	0.0238	0.0263	42.013	38.020

0.5%

Period n	Single Payment		Uniform Payment Series			
	Compound Amount Factor	Present Value Factor	Sinking Fund Factor	Capital Recovery Factor	Compound Amount Factor	Present Value Factor
	Find F Given P F/P	Find P Given F P/F	Find A Given F A/F	Find A Given P A/P	Find F Given A F/A	Find P Given A P/A
1	1.005	0.9950	1.0000	1.0050	1.000	0.995
2	1.010	0.9901	0.4988	0.5038	2.005	1.985
3	1.015	0.9851	0.3317	0.3367	3.015	2.970
4	1.020	0.9802	0.2481	0.2531	4.030	3.950
5	1.025	0.9754	0.1980	0.2030	5.050	4.926
6	1.030	0.9705	0.1646	0.1696	6.076	5.896
7	1.036	0.9657	0.1407	0.1457	7.106	6.862
8	1.041	0.9609	0.1228	0.1278	8.141	7.823
9	1.046	0.9561	0.1089	0.1139	9.182	8.779
10	1.051	0.9513	0.0978	0.1028	10.228	9.730
11	1.056	0.9466	0.0887	0.0937	11.279	10.677
12	1.062	0.9419	0.0811	0.0861	12.336	11.619
13	1.067	0.9372	0.0746	0.0796	13.397	12.556
14	1.072	0.9326	0.0691	0.0741	14.464	13.489
15	1.078	0.9279	0.0644	0.0694	15.537	14.417
16	1.083	0.9233	0.0602	0.0652	16.614	15.340
17	1.088	0.9187	0.0565	0.0615	17.697	16.259
18	1.094	0.9141	0.0532	0.0582	18.786	17.173
19	1.099	0.9096	0.0503	0.0553	19.880	18.082
20	1.105	0.9051	0.0477	0.0527	20.979	18.987
21	1.110	0.9006	0.0453	0.0503	22.084	19.888
22	1.116	0.8961	0.0431	0.0481	23.194	20.784
23	1.122	0.8916	0.0411	0.0461	24.310	21.676
24	1.127	0.8872	0.0393	0.0443	25.432	22.563
25	1.133	0.8828	0.0377	0.0427	26.559	23.446
26	1.138	0.8784	0.0361	0.0411	27.692	24.324
27	1.144	0.8740	0.0347	0.0397	28.830	25.198
28	1.150	0.8697	0.0334	0.0384	29.975	26.068
29	1.156	0.8653	0.0321	0.0371	31.124	26.933
30	1.161	0.8610	0.0310	0.0360	32.280	27.794
31	1.167	0.8567	0.0299	0.0349	33.441	28.651
32	1.173	0.8525	0.0289	0.0339	34.609	29.503
33	1.179	0.8482	0.0279	0.0329	35.782	30.352
34	1.185	0.8440	0.0271	0.0321	36.961	31.196
35	1.191	0.8398	0.0262	0.0312	38.145	32.035
36	1.197	0.8356	0.0254	0.0304	39.336	32.871
37	1.203	0.8315	0.0247	0.0297	40.533	33.703
38	1.209	0.8274	0.0240	0.0290	41.735	34.530
39	1.215	0.8232	0.0233	0.0283	42.944	35.353
40	1.221	0.8191	0.0226	0.0276	44.159	36.172

0.75%

	Single Payment		Uniform Payment Series			
	Compound Amount Factor	Present Value Factor	Sinking Fund Factor	Capital Recovery Factor	Compound Amount Factor	Present Value Factor
	Find F	Find P	Find A	Find A	Find F	Find P
Period	Given P	Given F	Given F	Given P	Given A	Given A
n	F/P	P/F	A/F	A/P	F/A	P/A
1	1.008	0.9926	1.0000	1.0075	1.000	0.993
2	1.015	0.9852	0.4981	0.5056	2.008	1.978
3	1.023	0.9778	0.3308	0.3383	3.023	2.956
4	1.030	0.9706	0.2472	0.2547	4.045	3.926
5	1.038	0.9633	0.1970	0.2045	5.076	4.889
6	1.046	0.9562	0.1636	0.1711	6.114	5.846
7	1.054	0.9490	0.1397	0.1472	7.159	6.795
8	1.062	0.9420	0.1218	0.1293	8.213	7.737
9	1.070	0.9350	0.1078	0.1153	9.275	8.672
10	1.078	0.9280	0.0967	0.1042	10.344	9.600
11	1.086	0.9211	0.0876	0.0951	11.422	10.521
12	1.094	0.9142	0.0800	0.0875	12.508	11.435
13	1.102	0.9074	0.0735	0.0810	13.601	12.342
14	1.110	0.9007	0.0680	0.0755	14.703	13.243
15	1.119	0.8940	0.0632	0.0707	15.814	14.137
16	1.127	0.8873	0.0591	0.0666	16.932	15.024
17	1.135	0.8807	0.0554	0.0629	18.059	15.905
18	1.144	0.8742	0.0521	0.0596	19.195	16.779
19	1.153	0.8676	0.0492	0.0567	20.339	17.647
20	1.161	0.8612	0.0465	0.0540	21.491	18.508
21	1.170	0.8548	0.0441	0.0516	22.652	19.363
22	1.179	0.8484	0.0420	0.0495	23.822	20.211
23	1.188	0.8421	0.0400	0.0475	25.001	21.053
24	1.196	0.8358	0.0382	0.0457	26.188	21.889
25	1.205	0.8296	0.0365	0.0440	27.385	22.719
26	1.214	0.8234	0.0350	0.0425	28.590	23.542
27	1.224	0.8173	0.0336	0.0411	29.805	24.359
28	1.233	0.8112	0.0322	0.0397	31.028	25.171
29	1.242	0.8052	0.0310	0.0385	32.261	25.976
30	1.251	0.7992	0.0298	0.0373	33.503	26.775
31	1.261	0.7932	0.0288	0.0363	34.754	27.568
32	1.270	0.7873	0.0278	0.0353	36.015	28.356
33	1.280	0.7815	0.0268	0.0343	37.285	29.137
34	1.289	0.7757	0.0259	0.0334	38.565	29.913
35	1.299	0.7699	0.0251	0.0326	39.854	30.683
36	1.309	0.7641	0.0243	0.0318	41.153	31.447
37	1.318	0.7585	0.0236	0.0311	42.461	32.205
38	1.328	0.7528	0.0228	0.0303	43.780	32.958
39	1.338	0.7472	0.0222	0.0297	45.108	33.705
40	1.348	0.7416	0.0215	0.0290	46.446	34.447

1%						
	Single Payment		**Uniform Payment Series**			
	Compound Amount Factor	Present Value Factor	Sinking Fund Factor	Capital Recovery Factor	Compound Amount Factor	Present Value Factor
Period *n*	Find *F* Given *P* *F/P*	Find *P* Given *F* *P/F*	Find *A* Given *F* *A/F*	Find *A* Given *P* *A/P*	Find *F* Given *A* *F/A*	Find *P* Given *A* *P/A*
1	1.010	0.9901	1.0000	1.0100	1.000	0.990
2	1.020	0.9803	0.4975	0.5075	2.010	1.970
3	1.030	0.9706	0.3300	0.3400	3.030	2.941
4	1.041	0.9610	0.2463	0.2563	4.060	3.902
5	1.051	0.9515	0.1960	0.2060	5.101	4.853
6	1.062	0.9420	0.1625	0.1725	6.152	5.795
7	1.072	0.9327	0.1386	0.1486	7.214	6.728
8	1.083	0.9235	0.1207	0.1307	8.286	7.652
9	1.094	0.9143	0.1067	0.1167	9.369	8.566
10	1.105	0.9053	0.0956	0.1056	10.462	9.471
11	1.116	0.8963	0.0865	0.0965	11.567	10.368
12	1.127	0.8874	0.0788	0.0888	12.683	11.255
13	1.138	0.8787	0.0724	0.0824	13.809	12.134
14	1.149	0.8700	0.0669	0.0769	14.947	13.004
15	1.161	0.8613	0.0621	0.0721	16.097	13.865
16	1.173	0.8528	0.0579	0.0679	17.258	14.718
17	1.184	0.8444	0.0543	0.0643	18.430	15.562
18	1.196	0.8360	0.0510	0.0610	19.615	16.398
19	1.208	0.8277	0.0481	0.0581	20.811	17.226
20	1.220	0.8195	0.0454	0.0554	22.019	18.046
21	1.232	0.8114	0.0430	0.0530	23.239	18.857
22	1.245	0.8034	0.0409	0.0509	24.472	19.660
23	1.257	0.7954	0.0389	0.0489	25.716	20.456
24	1.270	0.7876	0.0371	0.0471	26.973	21.243
25	1.282	0.7798	0.0354	0.0454	28.243	22.023
26	1.295	0.7720	0.0339	0.0439	29.526	22.795
27	1.308	0.7644	0.0324	0.0424	30.821	23.560
28	1.321	0.7568	0.0311	0.0411	32.129	24.316
29	1.335	0.7493	0.0299	0.0399	33.450	25.066
30	1.348	0.7419	0.0287	0.0387	34.785	25.808
31	1.361	0.7346	0.0277	0.0377	36.133	26.542
32	1.375	0.7273	0.0267	0.0367	37.494	27.270
33	1.389	0.7201	0.0257	0.0357	38.869	27.990
34	1.403	0.7130	0.0248	0.0348	40.258	28.703
35	1.417	0.7059	0.0240	0.0340	41.660	29.409
36	1.431	0.6989	0.0232	0.0332	43.077	30.108
37	1.445	0.6920	0.0225	0.0325	44.508	30.800
38	1.460	0.6852	0.0218	0.0318	45.953	31.485
39	1.474	0.6784	0.0211	0.0311	47.412	32.163
40	1.489	0.6717	0.0205	0.0305	48.886	32.835

1.25%						
	Single Payment		**Uniform Payment Series**			
	Compound Amount Factor	Present Value Factor	Sinking Fund Factor	Capital Recovery Factor	Compound Amount Factor	Present Value Factor
Period *n*	Find *F* Given *P* *F/P*	Find *P* Given *F* *P/F*	Find *A* Given *F* *A/F*	Find *A* Given *P* *A/P*	Find *F* Given *A* *F/A*	Find *P* Given *A* *P/A*
1	1.013	0.9877	1.0000	1.0125	1.000	0.988
2	1.025	0.9755	0.4969	0.5094	2.013	1.963
3	1.038	0.9634	0.3292	0.3417	3.038	2.927
4	1.051	0.9515	0.2454	0.2579	4.076	3.878
5	1.064	0.9398	0.1951	0.2076	5.127	4.818
6	1.077	0.9282	0.1615	0.1740	6.191	5.746
7	1.091	0.9167	0.1376	0.1501	7.268	6.663
8	1.104	0.9054	0.1196	0.1321	8.359	7.568
9	1.118	0.8942	0.1057	0.1182	9.463	8.462
10	1.132	0.8832	0.0945	0.1070	10.582	9.346
11	1.146	0.8723	0.0854	0.0979	11.714	10.218
12	1.161	0.8615	0.0778	0.0903	12.860	11.079
13	1.175	0.8509	0.0713	0.0838	14.021	11.930
14	1.190	0.8404	0.0658	0.0783	15.196	12.771
15	1.205	0.8300	0.0610	0.0735	16.386	13.601
16	1.220	0.8197	0.0568	0.0693	17.591	14.420
17	1.235	0.8096	0.0532	0.0657	18.811	15.230
18	1.251	0.7996	0.0499	0.0624	20.046	16.030
19	1.266	0.7898	0.0470	0.0595	21.297	16.819
20	1.282	0.7800	0.0443	0.0568	22.563	17.599
21	1.298	0.7704	0.0419	0.0544	23.845	18.370
22	1.314	0.7609	0.0398	0.0523	25.143	19.131
23	1.331	0.7515	0.0378	0.0503	26.457	19.882
24	1.347	0.7422	0.0360	0.0485	27.788	20.624
25	1.364	0.7330	0.0343	0.0468	29.135	21.357
26	1.381	0.7240	0.0328	0.0453	30.500	22.081
27	1.399	0.7150	0.0314	0.0439	31.881	22.796
28	1.416	0.7062	0.0300	0.0425	33.279	23.503
29	1.434	0.6975	0.0288	0.0413	34.695	24.200
30	1.452	0.6889	0.0277	0.0402	36.129	24.889
31	1.470	0.6804	0.0266	0.0391	37.581	25.569
32	1.488	0.6720	0.0256	0.0381	39.050	26.241
33	1.507	0.6637	0.0247	0.0372	40.539	26.905
34	1.526	0.6555	0.0238	0.0363	42.045	27.560
35	1.545	0.6474	0.0230	0.0355	43.571	28.208
36	1.564	0.6394	0.0222	0.0347	45.116	28.847
37	1.583	0.6315	0.0214	0.0339	46.679	29.479
38	1.603	0.6237	0.0207	0.0332	48.263	30.103
39	1.623	0.6160	0.0201	0.0326	49.866	30.719
40	1.644	0.6084	0.0194	0.0319	51.490	31.327

1.5%	Single Payment		Uniform Payment Series			
	Compound Amount Factor	Present Value Factor	Sinking Fund Factor	Capital Recovery Factor	Compound Amount Factor	Present Value Factor
Period *n*	Find *F* Given *P* F/P	Find *P* Given *F* P/F	Find *A* Given *F* A/F	Find *A* Given *P* A/P	Find *F* Given *A* F/A	Find *P* Given *A* P/A
1	1.015	0.9852	1.0000	1.0150	1.000	0.985
2	1.030	0.9707	0.4963	0.5113	2.015	1.956
3	1.046	0.9563	0.3284	0.3434	3.045	2.912
4	1.061	0.9422	0.2444	0.2594	4.091	3.854
5	1.077	0.9283	0.1941	0.2091	5.152	4.783
6	1.093	0.9145	0.1605	0.1755	6.230	5.697
7	1.110	0.9010	0.1366	0.1516	7.323	6.598
8	1.126	0.8877	0.1186	0.1336	8.433	7.486
9	1.143	0.8746	0.1046	0.1196	9.559	8.361
10	1.161	0.8617	0.0934	0.1084	10.703	9.222
11	1.178	0.8489	0.0843	0.0993	11.863	10.071
12	1.196	0.8364	0.0767	0.0917	13.041	10.908
13	1.214	0.8240	0.0702	0.0852	14.237	11.732
14	1.232	0.8118	0.0647	0.0797	15.450	12.543
15	1.250	0.7999	0.0599	0.0749	16.682	13.343
16	1.269	0.7880	0.0558	0.0708	17.932	14.131
17	1.288	0.7764	0.0521	0.0671	19.201	14.908
18	1.307	0.7649	0.0488	0.0638	20.489	15.673
19	1.327	0.7536	0.0459	0.0609	21.797	16.426
20	1.347	0.7425	0.0432	0.0582	23.124	17.169
21	1.367	0.7315	0.0409	0.0559	24.471	17.900
22	1.388	0.7207	0.0387	0.0537	25.838	18.621
23	1.408	0.7100	0.0367	0.0517	27.225	19.331
24	1.430	0.6995	0.0349	0.0499	28.634	20.030
25	1.451	0.6892	0.0333	0.0483	30.063	20.720
26	1.473	0.6790	0.0317	0.0467	31.514	21.399
27	1.495	0.6690	0.0303	0.0453	32.987	22.068
28	1.517	0.6591	0.0290	0.0440	34.481	22.727
29	1.540	0.6494	0.0278	0.0428	35.999	23.376
30	1.563	0.6398	0.0266	0.0416	37.539	24.016
31	1.587	0.6303	0.0256	0.0406	39.102	24.646
32	1.610	0.6210	0.0246	0.0396	40.688	25.267
33	1.634	0.6118	0.0236	0.0386	42.299	25.879
34	1.659	0.6028	0.0228	0.0378	43.933	26.482
35	1.684	0.5939	0.0219	0.0369	45.592	27.076
36	1.709	0.5851	0.0212	0.0362	47.276	27.661
37	1.735	0.5764	0.0204	0.0354	48.985	28.237
38	1.761	0.5679	0.0197	0.0347	50.720	28.805
39	1.787	0.5595	0.0191	0.0341	52.481	29.365
40	1.814	0.5513	0.0184	0.0334	54.268	29.916

1.75%						
	Single Payment		**Uniform Payment Series**			
	Compound Amount Factor	**Present Value Factor**	**Sinking Fund Factor**	**Capital Recovery Factor**	**Compound Amount Factor**	**Present Value Factor**
Period **n**	**Find F Given P** F/P	**Find P Given F** P/F	**Find A Given F** A/F	**Find A Given P** A/P	**Find F Given A** F/A	**Find P Given A** P/A
1	1.018	0.9828	1.0000	1.0175	1.000	0.983
2	1.035	0.9659	0.4957	0.5132	2.018	1.949
3	1.053	0.9493	0.3276	0.3451	3.053	2.898
4	1.072	0.9330	0.2435	0.2610	4.106	3.831
5	1.091	0.9169	0.1931	0.2106	5.178	4.748
6	1.110	0.9011	0.1595	0.1770	6.269	5.649
7	1.129	0.8856	0.1355	0.1530	7.378	6.535
8	1.149	0.8704	0.1175	0.1350	8.508	7.405
9	1.169	0.8554	0.1036	0.1211	9.656	8.260
10	1.189	0.8407	0.0924	0.1099	10.825	9.101
11	1.210	0.8263	0.0832	0.1007	12.015	9.927
12	1.231	0.8121	0.0756	0.0931	13.225	10.740
13	1.253	0.7981	0.0692	0.0867	14.457	11.538
14	1.275	0.7844	0.0637	0.0812	15.710	12.322
15	1.297	0.7709	0.0589	0.0764	16.984	13.093
16	1.320	0.7576	0.0547	0.0722	18.282	13.850
17	1.343	0.7446	0.0510	0.0685	19.602	14.595
18	1.367	0.7318	0.0477	0.0652	20.945	15.327
19	1.390	0.7192	0.0448	0.0623	22.311	16.046
20	1.415	0.7068	0.0422	0.0597	23.702	16.753
21	1.440	0.6947	0.0398	0.0573	25.116	17.448
22	1.465	0.6827	0.0377	0.0552	26.556	18.130
23	1.490	0.6710	0.0357	0.0532	28.021	18.801
24	1.516	0.6594	0.0339	0.0514	29.511	19.461
25	1.543	0.6481	0.0322	0.0497	31.027	20.109
26	1.570	0.6369	0.0307	0.0482	32.570	20.746
27	1.597	0.6260	0.0293	0.0468	34.140	21.372
28	1.625	0.6152	0.0280	0.0455	35.738	21.987
29	1.654	0.6046	0.0268	0.0443	37.363	22.592
30	1.683	0.5942	0.0256	0.0431	39.017	23.186
31	1.712	0.5840	0.0246	0.0421	40.700	23.770
32	1.742	0.5740	0.0236	0.0411	42.412	24.344
33	1.773	0.5641	0.0226	0.0401	44.154	24.908
34	1.804	0.5544	0.0218	0.0393	45.927	25.462
35	1.835	0.5449	0.0210	0.0385	47.731	26.007
36	1.867	0.5355	0.0202	0.0377	49.566	26.543
37	1.900	0.5263	0.0194	0.0369	51.434	27.069
38	1.933	0.5172	0.0187	0.0362	53.334	27.586
39	1.967	0.5083	0.0181	0.0356	55.267	28.095
40	2.002	0.4996	0.0175	0.0350	57.234	28.594

2%	Single Payment		Uniform Payment Series			
	Compound Amount Factor	Present Value Factor	Sinking Fund Factor	Capital Recovery Factor	Compound Amount Factor	Present Value Factor
Period n	Find F Given P F/P	Find P Given F P/F	Find A Given F A/F	Find A Given P A/P	Find F Given A F/A	Find P Given A P/A
1	1.020	0.9804	1.0000	1.0200	1.000	0.980
2	1.040	0.9612	0.4950	0.5150	2.020	1.942
3	1.061	0.9423	0.3268	0.3468	3.060	2.884
4	1.082	0.9238	0.2426	0.2626	4.122	3.808
5	1.104	0.9057	0.1922	0.2122	5.204	4.713
6	1.126	0.8880	0.1585	0.1785	6.308	5.601
7	1.149	0.8706	0.1345	0.1545	7.434	6.472
8	1.172	0.8535	0.1165	0.1365	8.583	7.325
9	1.195	0.8368	0.1025	0.1225	9.755	8.162
10	1.219	0.8203	0.0913	0.1113	10.950	8.983
11	1.243	0.8043	0.0822	0.1022	12.169	9.787
12	1.268	0.7885	0.0746	0.0946	13.412	10.575
13	1.294	0.7730	0.0681	0.0881	14.680	11.348
14	1.319	0.7579	0.0626	0.0826	15.974	12.106
15	1.346	0.7430	0.0578	0.0778	17.293	12.849
16	1.373	0.7284	0.0537	0.0737	18.639	13.578
17	1.400	0.7142	0.0500	0.0700	20.012	14.292
18	1.428	0.7002	0.0467	0.0667	21.412	14.992
19	1.457	0.6864	0.0438	0.0638	22.841	15.678
20	1.486	0.6730	0.0412	0.0612	24.297	16.351
21	1.516	0.6598	0.0388	0.0588	25.783	17.011
22	1.546	0.6468	0.0366	0.0566	27.299	17.658
23	1.577	0.6342	0.0347	0.0547	28.845	18.292
24	1.608	0.6217	0.0329	0.0529	30.422	18.914
25	1.641	0.6095	0.0312	0.0512	32.030	19.523
26	1.673	0.5976	0.0297	0.0497	33.671	20.121
27	1.707	0.5859	0.0283	0.0483	35.344	20.707
28	1.741	0.5744	0.0270	0.0470	37.051	21.281
29	1.776	0.5631	0.0258	0.0458	38.792	21.844
30	1.811	0.5521	0.0246	0.0446	40.568	22.396
31	1.848	0.5412	0.0236	0.0436	42.379	22.938
32	1.885	0.5306	0.0226	0.0426	44.227	23.468
33	1.922	0.5202	0.0217	0.0417	46.112	23.989
34	1.961	0.5100	0.0208	0.0408	48.034	24.499
35	2.000	0.5000	0.0200	0.0400	49.994	24.999
36	2.040	0.4902	0.0192	0.0392	51.994	25.489
37	2.081	0.4806	0.0185	0.0385	54.034	25.969
38	2.122	0.4712	0.0178	0.0378	56.115	26.441
39	2.165	0.4619	0.0172	0.0372	58.237	26.903
40	2.208	0.4529	0.0166	0.0366	60.402	27.355

2.5%	Single Payment		Uniform Payment Series			
	Compound Amount Factor	Present Value Factor	Sinking Fund Factor	Capital Recovery Factor	Compound Amount Factor	Present Value Factor
	Find F Given P	Find P Given F	Find A Given F	Find A Given P	Find F Given A	Find P Given A
Period n	F/P	P/F	A/F	A/P	F/A	P/A
1	1.025	0.9756	1.0000	1.0250	1.000	0.976
2	1.051	0.9518	0.4938	0.5188	2.025	1.927
3	1.077	0.9286	0.3251	0.3501	3.076	2.856
4	1.104	0.9060	0.2408	0.2658	4.153	3.762
5	1.131	0.8839	0.1902	0.2152	5.256	4.646
6	1.160	0.8623	0.1565	0.1815	6.388	5.508
7	1.189	0.8413	0.1325	0.1575	7.547	6.349
8	1.218	0.8207	0.1145	0.1395	8.736	7.170
9	1.249	0.8007	0.1005	0.1255	9.955	7.971
10	1.280	0.7812	0.0893	0.1143	11.203	8.752
11	1.312	0.7621	0.0801	0.1051	12.483	9.514
12	1.345	0.7436	0.0725	0.0975	13.796	10.258
13	1.379	0.7254	0.0660	0.0910	15.140	10.983
14	1.413	0.7077	0.0605	0.0855	16.519	11.691
15	1.448	0.6905	0.0558	0.0808	17.932	12.381
16	1.485	0.6736	0.0516	0.0766	19.380	13.055
17	1.522	0.6572	0.0479	0.0729	20.865	13.712
18	1.560	0.6412	0.0447	0.0697	22.386	14.353
19	1.599	0.6255	0.0418	0.0668	23.946	14.979
20	1.639	0.6103	0.0391	0.0641	25.545	15.589
21	1.680	0.5954	0.0368	0.0618	27.183	16.185
22	1.722	0.5809	0.0346	0.0596	28.863	16.765
23	1.765	0.5667	0.0327	0.0577	30.584	17.332
24	1.809	0.5529	0.0309	0.0559	32.349	17.885
25	1.854	0.5394	0.0293	0.0543	34.158	18.424
26	1.900	0.5262	0.0278	0.0528	36.012	18.951
27	1.948	0.5134	0.0264	0.0514	37.912	19.464
28	1.996	0.5009	0.0251	0.0501	39.860	19.965
29	2.046	0.4887	0.0239	0.0489	41.856	20.454
30	2.098	0.4767	0.0228	0.0478	43.903	20.930
31	2.150	0.4651	0.0217	0.0467	46.000	21.395
32	2.204	0.4538	0.0208	0.0458	48.150	21.849
33	2.259	0.4427	0.0199	0.0449	50.354	22.292
34	2.315	0.4319	0.0190	0.0440	52.613	22.724
35	2.373	0.4214	0.0182	0.0432	54.928	23.145
36	2.433	0.4111	0.0175	0.0425	57.301	23.556
37	2.493	0.4011	0.0167	0.0417	59.734	23.957
38	2.556	0.3913	0.0161	0.0411	62.227	24.349
39	2.620	0.3817	0.0154	0.0404	64.783	24.730
40	2.685	0.3724	0.0148	0.0398	67.403	25.103

3%	Single Payment		Uniform Payment Series			
	Compound Amount Factor	Present Value Factor	Sinking Fund Factor	Capital Recovery Factor	Compound Amount Factor	Present Value Factor
Period n	Find F Given P F/P	Find P Given F P/F	Find A Given F A/F	Find A Given P A/P	Find F Given A F/A	Find P Given A P/A
1	1.030	0.9709	1.0000	1.0300	1.000	0.971
2	1.061	0.9426	0.4926	0.5226	2.030	1.913
3	1.093	0.9151	0.3235	0.3535	3.091	2.829
4	1.126	0.8885	0.2390	0.2690	4.184	3.717
5	1.159	0.8626	0.1884	0.2184	5.309	4.580
6	1.194	0.8375	0.1546	0.1846	6.468	5.417
7	1.230	0.8131	0.1305	0.1605	7.662	6.230
8	1.267	0.7894	0.1125	0.1425	8.892	7.020
9	1.305	0.7664	0.0984	0.1284	10.159	7.786
10	1.344	0.7441	0.0872	0.1172	11.464	8.530
11	1.384	0.7224	0.0781	0.1081	12.808	9.253
12	1.426	0.7014	0.0705	0.1005	14.192	9.954
13	1.469	0.6810	0.0640	0.0940	15.618	10.635
14	1.513	0.6611	0.0585	0.0885	17.086	11.296
15	1.558	0.6419	0.0538	0.0838	18.599	11.938
16	1.605	0.6232	0.0496	0.0796	20.157	12.561
17	1.653	0.6050	0.0460	0.0760	21.762	13.166
18	1.702	0.5874	0.0427	0.0727	23.414	13.754
19	1.754	0.5703	0.0398	0.0698	25.117	14.324
20	1.806	0.5537	0.0372	0.0672	26.870	14.877
21	1.860	0.5375	0.0349	0.0649	28.676	15.415
22	1.916	0.5219	0.0327	0.0627	30.537	15.937
23	1.974	0.5067	0.0308	0.0608	32.453	16.444
24	2.033	0.4919	0.0290	0.0590	34.426	16.936
25	2.094	0.4776	0.0274	0.0574	36.459	17.413
26	2.157	0.4637	0.0259	0.0559	38.553	17.877
27	2.221	0.4502	0.0246	0.0546	40.710	18.327
28	2.288	0.4371	0.0233	0.0533	42.931	18.764
29	2.357	0.4243	0.0221	0.0521	45.219	19.188
30	2.427	0.4120	0.0210	0.0510	47.575	19.600
31	2.500	0.4000	0.0200	0.0500	50.003	20.000
32	2.575	0.3883	0.0190	0.0490	52.503	20.389
33	2.652	0.3770	0.0182	0.0482	55.078	20.766
34	2.732	0.3660	0.0173	0.0473	57.730	21.132
35	2.814	0.3554	0.0165	0.0465	60.462	21.487
36	2.898	0.3450	0.0158	0.0458	63.276	21.832
37	2.985	0.3350	0.0151	0.0451	66.174	22.167
38	3.075	0.3252	0.0145	0.0445	69.159	22.492
39	3.167	0.3158	0.0138	0.0438	72.234	22.808
40	3.262	0.3066	0.0133	0.0433	75.401	23.115

3.5%	Single Payment		Uniform Payment Series			
	Compound Amount Factor	Present Value Factor	Sinking Fund Factor	Capital Recovery Factor	Compound Amount Factor	Present Value Factor
Period *n*	Find *F* Given *P* F/P	Find *P* Given *F* P/F	Find *A* Given *F* A/F	Find *A* Given *P* A/P	Find *F* Given *A* F/A	Find *P* Given *A* P/A
1	1.035	0.9662	1.0000	1.0350	1.000	0.966
2	1.071	0.9335	0.4914	0.5264	2.035	1.900
3	1.109	0.9019	0.3219	0.3569	3.106	2.802
4	1.148	0.8714	0.2373	0.2723	4.215	3.673
5	1.188	0.8420	0.1865	0.2215	5.362	4.515
6	1.229	0.8135	0.1527	0.1877	6.550	5.329
7	1.272	0.7860	0.1285	0.1635	7.779	6.115
8	1.317	0.7594	0.1105	0.1455	9.052	6.874
9	1.363	0.7337	0.0964	0.1314	10.368	7.608
10	1.411	0.7089	0.0852	0.1202	11.731	8.317
11	1.460	0.6849	0.0761	0.1111	13.142	9.002
12	1.511	0.6618	0.0685	0.1035	14.602	9.663
13	1.564	0.6394	0.0621	0.0971	16.113	10.303
14	1.619	0.6178	0.0566	0.0916	17.677	10.921
15	1.675	0.5969	0.0518	0.0868	19.296	11.517
16	1.734	0.5767	0.0477	0.0827	20.971	12.094
17	1.795	0.5572	0.0440	0.0790	22.705	12.651
18	1.857	0.5384	0.0408	0.0758	24.500	13.190
19	1.923	0.5202	0.0379	0.0729	26.357	13.710
20	1.990	0.5026	0.0354	0.0704	28.280	14.212
21	2.059	0.4856	0.0330	0.0680	30.269	14.698
22	2.132	0.4692	0.0309	0.0659	32.329	15.167
23	2.206	0.4533	0.0290	0.0640	34.460	15.620
24	2.283	0.4380	0.0273	0.0623	36.667	16.058
25	2.363	0.4231	0.0257	0.0607	38.950	16.482
26	2.446	0.4088	0.0242	0.0592	41.313	16.890
27	2.532	0.3950	0.0229	0.0579	43.759	17.285
28	2.620	0.3817	0.0216	0.0566	46.291	17.667
29	2.712	0.3687	0.0204	0.0554	48.911	18.036
30	2.807	0.3563	0.0194	0.0544	51.623	18.392
31	2.905	0.3442	0.0184	0.0534	54.429	18.736
32	3.007	0.3326	0.0174	0.0524	57.335	19.069
33	3.112	0.3213	0.0166	0.0516	60.341	19.390
34	3.221	0.3105	0.0158	0.0508	63.453	19.701
35	3.334	0.3000	0.0150	0.0500	66.674	20.001
36	3.450	0.2898	0.0143	0.0493	70.008	20.290
37	3.571	0.2800	0.0136	0.0486	73.458	20.571
38	3.696	0.2706	0.0130	0.0480	77.029	20.841
39	3.825	0.2614	0.0124	0.0474	80.725	21.102
40	3.959	0.2526	0.0118	0.0468	84.550	21.355

4%	Single Payment		Uniform Payment Series			
	Compound Amount Factor	Present Value Factor	Sinking Fund Factor	Capital Recovery Factor	Compound Amount Factor	Present Value Factor
	Find F	Find P	Find A	Find A	Find F	Find P
Period	Given P	Given F	Given F	Given P	Given A	Given A
n	F/P	P/F	A/F	A/P	F/A	P/A
1	1.040	0.9615	1.0000	1.0400	1.000	0.962
2	1.082	0.9246	0.4902	0.5302	2.040	1.886
3	1.125	0.8890	0.3203	0.3603	3.122	2.775
4	1.170	0.8548	0.2355	0.2755	4.246	3.630
5	1.217	0.8219	0.1846	0.2246	5.416	4.452
6	1.265	0.7903	0.1508	0.1908	6.633	5.242
7	1.316	0.7599	0.1266	0.1666	7.898	6.002
8	1.369	0.7307	0.1085	0.1485	9.214	6.733
9	1.423	0.7026	0.0945	0.1345	10.583	7.435
10	1.480	0.6756	0.0833	0.1233	12.006	8.111
11	1.539	0.6496	0.0741	0.1141	13.486	8.760
12	1.601	0.6246	0.0666	0.1066	15.026	9.385
13	1.665	0.6006	0.0601	0.1001	16.627	9.986
14	1.732	0.5775	0.0547	0.0947	18.292	10.563
15	1.801	0.5553	0.0499	0.0899	20.024	11.118
16	1.873	0.5339	0.0458	0.0858	21.825	11.652
17	1.948	0.5134	0.0422	0.0822	23.698	12.166
18	2.026	0.4936	0.0390	0.0790	25.645	12.659
19	2.107	0.4746	0.0361	0.0761	27.671	13.134
20	2.191	0.4564	0.0336	0.0736	29.778	13.590
21	2.279	0.4388	0.0313	0.0713	31.969	14.029
22	2.370	0.4220	0.0292	0.0692	34.248	14.451
23	2.465	0.4057	0.0273	0.0673	36.618	14.857
24	2.563	0.3901	0.0256	0.0656	39.083	15.247
25	2.666	0.3751	0.0240	0.0640	41.646	15.622
26	2.772	0.3607	0.0226	0.0626	44.312	15.983
27	2.883	0.3468	0.0212	0.0612	47.084	16.330
28	2.999	0.3335	0.0200	0.0600	49.968	16.663
29	3.119	0.3207	0.0189	0.0589	52.966	16.984
30	3.243	0.3083	0.0178	0.0578	56.085	17.292
31	3.373	0.2965	0.0169	0.0569	59.328	17.588
32	3.508	0.2851	0.0159	0.0559	62.701	17.874
33	3.648	0.2741	0.0151	0.0551	66.210	18.148
34	3.794	0.2636	0.0143	0.0543	69.858	18.411
35	3.946	0.2534	0.0136	0.0536	73.652	18.665
36	4.104	0.2437	0.0129	0.0529	77.598	18.908
37	4.268	0.2343	0.0122	0.0522	81.702	19.143
38	4.439	0.2253	0.0116	0.0516	85.970	19.368
39	4.616	0.2166	0.0111	0.0511	90.409	19.584
40	4.801	0.2083	0.0105	0.0505	95.026	19.793

4.5%						
	Single Payment		**Uniform Payment Series**			
	Compound Amount Factor	Present Value Factor	Sinking Fund Factor	Capital Recovery Factor	Compound Amount Factor	Present Value Factor
Period n	Find F Given P F/P	Find P Given F P/F	Find A Given F A/F	Find A Given P A/P	Find F Given A F/A	Find P Given A P/A
1	1.045	0.9569	1.0000	1.0450	1.000	0.957
2	1.092	0.9157	0.4890	0.5340	2.045	1.873
3	1.141	0.8763	0.3188	0.3638	3.137	2.749
4	1.193	0.8386	0.2337	0.2787	4.278	3.588
5	1.246	0.8025	0.1828	0.2278	5.471	4.390
6	1.302	0.7679	0.1489	0.1939	6.717	5.158
7	1.361	0.7348	0.1247	0.1697	8.019	5.893
8	1.422	0.7032	0.1066	0.1516	9.380	6.596
9	1.486	0.6729	0.0926	0.1376	10.802	7.269
10	1.553	0.6439	0.0814	0.1264	12.288	7.913
11	1.623	0.6162	0.0722	0.1172	13.841	8.529
12	1.696	0.5897	0.0647	0.1097	15.464	9.119
13	1.772	0.5643	0.0583	0.1033	17.160	9.683
14	1.852	0.5400	0.0528	0.0978	18.932	10.223
15	1.935	0.5167	0.0481	0.0931	20.784	10.740
16	2.022	0.4945	0.0440	0.0890	22.719	11.234
17	2.113	0.4732	0.0404	0.0854	24.742	11.707
18	2.208	0.4528	0.0372	0.0822	26.855	12.160
19	2.308	0.4333	0.0344	0.0794	29.064	12.593
20	2.412	0.4146	0.0319	0.0769	31.371	13.008
21	2.520	0.3968	0.0296	0.0746	33.783	13.405
22	2.634	0.3797	0.0275	0.0725	36.303	13.784
23	2.752	0.3634	0.0257	0.0707	38.937	14.148
24	2.876	0.3477	0.0240	0.0690	41.689	14.495
25	3.005	0.3327	0.0224	0.0674	44.565	14.828
26	3.141	0.3184	0.0210	0.0660	47.571	15.147
27	3.282	0.3047	0.0197	0.0647	50.711	15.451
28	3.430	0.2916	0.0185	0.0635	53.993	15.743
29	3.584	0.2790	0.0174	0.0624	57.423	16.022
30	3.745	0.2670	0.0164	0.0614	61.007	16.289
31	3.914	0.2555	0.0154	0.0604	64.752	16.544
32	4.090	0.2445	0.0146	0.0596	68.666	16.789
33	4.274	0.2340	0.0137	0.0587	72.756	17.023
34	4.466	0.2239	0.0130	0.0580	77.030	17.247
35	4.667	0.2143	0.0123	0.0573	81.497	17.461
36	4.877	0.2050	0.0116	0.0566	86.164	17.666
37	5.097	0.1962	0.0110	0.0560	91.041	17.862
38	5.326	0.1878	0.0104	0.0554	96.138	18.050
39	5.566	0.1797	0.0099	0.0549	101.464	18.230
40	5.816	0.1719	0.0093	0.0543	107.030	18.402

5%						
	Single Payment		**Uniform Payment Series**			
	Compound Amount Factor	Present Value Factor	Sinking Fund Factor	Capital Recovery Factor	Compound Amount Factor	Present Value Factor
	Find *F*	Find *P*	Find *A*	Find *A*	Find *F*	Find *P*
Period	Given *P*	Given *F*	Given *F*	Given *P*	Given *A*	Given *A*
n	*F/P*	*P/F*	*A/F*	*A/P*	*F/A*	*P/A*
1	1.050	0.9524	1.0000	1.0500	1.000	0.952
2	1.103	0.9070	0.4878	0.5378	2.050	1.859
3	1.158	0.8638	0.3172	0.3672	3.153	2.723
4	1.216	0.8227	0.2320	0.2820	4.310	3.546
5	1.276	0.7835	0.1810	0.2310	5.526	4.329
6	1.340	0.7462	0.1470	0.1970	6.802	5.076
7	1.407	0.7107	0.1228	0.1728	8.142	5.786
8	1.477	0.6768	0.1047	0.1547	9.549	6.463
9	1.551	0.6446	0.0907	0.1407	11.027	7.108
10	1.629	0.6139	0.0795	0.1295	12.578	7.722
11	1.710	0.5847	0.0704	0.1204	14.207	8.306
12	1.796	0.5568	0.0628	0.1128	15.917	8.863
13	1.886	0.5303	0.0565	0.1065	17.713	9.394
14	1.980	0.5051	0.0510	0.1010	19.599	9.899
15	2.079	0.4810	0.0463	0.0963	21.579	10.380
16	2.183	0.4581	0.0423	0.0923	23.657	10.838
17	2.292	0.4363	0.0387	0.0887	25.840	11.274
18	2.407	0.4155	0.0355	0.0855	28.132	11.690
19	2.527	0.3957	0.0327	0.0827	30.539	12.085
20	2.653	0.3769	0.0302	0.0802	33.066	12.462
21	2.786	0.3589	0.0280	0.0780	35.719	12.821
22	2.925	0.3418	0.0260	0.0760	38.505	13.163
23	3.072	0.3256	0.0241	0.0741	41.430	13.489
24	3.225	0.3101	0.0225	0.0725	44.502	13.799
25	3.386	0.2953	0.0210	0.0710	47.727	14.094
26	3.556	0.2812	0.0196	0.0696	51.113	14.375
27	3.733	0.2678	0.0183	0.0683	54.669	14.643
28	3.920	0.2551	0.0171	0.0671	58.403	14.898
29	4.116	0.2429	0.0160	0.0660	62.323	15.141
30	4.322	0.2314	0.0151	0.0651	66.439	15.372
31	4.538	0.2204	0.0141	0.0641	70.761	15.593
32	4.765	0.2099	0.0133	0.0633	75.299	15.803
33	5.003	0.1999	0.0125	0.0625	80.064	16.003
34	5.253	0.1904	0.0118	0.0618	85.067	16.193
35	5.516	0.1813	0.0111	0.0611	90.320	16.374
36	5.792	0.1727	0.0104	0.0604	95.836	16.547
37	6.081	0.1644	0.0098	0.0598	101.628	16.711
38	6.385	0.1566	0.0093	0.0593	107.710	16.868
39	6.705	0.1491	0.0088	0.0588	114.095	17.017
40	7.040	0.1420	0.0083	0.0583	120.800	17.159

10%	Single Payment		Uniform Payment Series			
	Compound Amount Factor	Present Value Factor	Sinking Fund Factor	Capital Recovery Factor	Compound Amount Factor	Present Value Factor
	Find F	Find P	Find A	Find A	Find F	Find P
Period	Given P	Given F	Given F	Given P	Given A	Given A
n	F/P	P/F	A/F	A/P	F/A	P/A
1	1.100	0.9091	1.0000	1.1000	1.000	0.909
2	1.210	0.8264	0.4762	0.5762	2.100	1.736
3	1.331	0.7513	0.3021	0.4021	3.310	2.487
4	1.464	0.6830	0.2155	0.3155	4.641	3.170
5	1.611	0.6209	0.1638	0.2638	6.105	3.791
6	1.772	0.5645	0.1296	0.2296	7.716	4.355
7	1.949	0.5132	0.1054	0.2054	9.487	4.868
8	2.144	0.4665	0.0874	0.1874	11.436	5.335
9	2.358	0.4241	0.0736	0.1736	13.579	5.759
10	2.594	0.3855	0.0627	0.1627	15.937	6.145
11	2.853	0.3505	0.0540	0.1540	18.531	6.495
12	3.138	0.3186	0.0468	0.1468	21.384	6.814
13	3.452	0.2897	0.0408	0.1408	24.523	7.103
14	3.797	0.2633	0.0357	0.1357	27.975	7.367
15	4.177	0.2394	0.0315	0.1315	31.772	7.606
16	4.595	0.2176	0.0278	0.1278	35.950	7.824
17	5.054	0.1978	0.0247	0.1247	40.545	8.022
18	5.560	0.1799	0.0219	0.1219	45.599	8.201
19	6.116	0.1635	0.0195	0.1195	51.159	8.365
20	6.727	0.1486	0.0175	0.1175	57.275	8.514
21	7.400	0.1351	0.0156	0.1156	64.002	8.649
22	8.140	0.1228	0.0140	0.1140	71.403	8.772
23	8.954	0.1117	0.0126	0.1126	79.543	8.883
24	9.850	0.1015	0.0113	0.1113	88.497	8.985
25	10.835	0.0923	0.0102	0.1102	98.347	9.077
26	11.918	0.0839	0.0092	0.1092	109.182	9.161
27	13.110	0.0763	0.0083	0.1083	121.100	9.237
28	14.421	0.0693	0.0075	0.1075	134.210	9.307
29	15.863	0.0630	0.0067	0.1067	148.631	9.370
30	17.449	0.0573	0.0061	0.1061	164.494	9.427
31	19.194	0.0521	0.0055	0.1055	181.943	9.479
32	21.114	0.0474	0.0050	0.1050	201.138	9.526
33	23.225	0.0431	0.0045	0.1045	222.252	9.569
34	25.548	0.0391	0.0041	0.1041	245.477	9.609
35	28.102	0.0356	0.0037	0.1037	271.024	9.644
36	30.913	0.0323	0.0033	0.1033	299.127	9.677
37	34.004	0.0294	0.0030	0.1030	330.039	9.706
38	37.404	0.0267	0.0027	0.1027	364.043	9.733
39	41.145	0.0243	0.0025	0.1025	401.448	9.757
40	45.259	0.0221	0.0023	0.1023	442.593	9.779

12%	Single Payment		Uniform Payment Series			
	Compound Amount Factor	Present Value Factor	Sinking Fund Factor	Capital Recovery Factor	Compound Amount Factor	Present Value Factor
Period *n*	Find *F* Given *P* *F/P*	Find *P* Given *F* *P/F*	Find *A* Given *F* *A/F*	Find *A* Given *P* *A/P*	Find *F* Given *A* *F/A*	Find *P* Given *A* *P/A*
1	1.120	0.8929	1.0000	1.1200	1.000	0.893
2	1.254	0.7972	0.4717	0.5917	2.120	1.690
3	1.405	0.7118	0.2963	0.4163	3.374	2.402
4	1.574	0.6355	0.2092	0.3292	4.779	3.037
5	1.762	0.5674	0.1574	0.2774	6.353	3.605
6	1.974	0.5066	0.1232	0.2432	8.115	4.111
7	2.211	0.4523	0.0991	0.2191	10.089	4.564
8	2.476	0.4039	0.0813	0.2013	12.300	4.968
9	2.773	0.3606	0.0677	0.1877	14.776	5.328
10	3.106	0.3220	0.0570	0.1770	17.549	5.650
11	3.479	0.2875	0.0484	0.1684	20.655	5.938
12	3.896	0.2567	0.0414	0.1614	24.133	6.194
13	4.363	0.2292	0.0357	0.1557	28.029	6.424
14	4.887	0.2046	0.0309	0.1509	32.393	6.628
15	5.474	0.1827	0.0268	0.1468	37.280	6.811
16	6.130	0.1631	0.0234	0.1434	42.753	6.974
17	6.866	0.1456	0.0205	0.1405	48.884	7.120
18	7.690	0.1300	0.0179	0.1379	55.750	7.250
19	8.613	0.1161	0.0158	0.1358	63.440	7.366
20	9.646	0.1037	0.0139	0.1339	72.052	7.469
21	10.804	0.0926	0.0122	0.1322	81.699	7.562
22	12.100	0.0826	0.0108	0.1308	92.503	7.645
23	13.552	0.0738	0.0096	0.1296	104.603	7.718
24	15.179	0.0659	0.0085	0.1285	118.155	7.784
25	17.000	0.0588	0.0075	0.1275	133.334	7.843
26	19.040	0.0525	0.0067	0.1267	150.334	7.896
27	21.325	0.0469	0.0059	0.1259	169.374	7.943
28	23.884	0.0419	0.0052	0.1252	190.699	7.984
29	26.750	0.0374	0.0047	0.1247	214.583	8.022
30	29.960	0.0334	0.0041	0.1241	241.333	8.055
31	33.555	0.0298	0.0037	0.1237	271.293	8.085
32	37.582	0.0266	0.0033	0.1233	304.848	8.112
33	42.092	0.0238	0.0029	0.1229	342.429	8.135
34	47.143	0.0212	0.0026	0.1226	384.521	8.157
35	52.800	0.0189	0.0023	0.1223	431.663	8.176
36	59.136	0.0169	0.0021	0.1221	484.463	8.192
37	66.232	0.0151	0.0018	0.1218	543.599	8.208
38	74.180	0.0135	0.0016	0.1216	609.831	8.221
39	83.081	0.0120	0.0015	0.1215	684.010	8.233
40	93.051	0.0107	0.0013	0.1213	767.091	8.244